Bicycling Fu

Bicycling Fuel

Nutrition for bicycle riders

Richard Rafoth MD

Bicycle Books – San Francisco

Second, revised and expanded edition 1989

Printed in the United States of America

Published by:
Bicycle Books, Inc.
PO Box 2038
Mill Valley CA 94941

Book and cover design and diagrams by Rob van der Plas
Cover photograph by Stief
Bicycle courtesy Fahrradgesellschaft, Offenbach, W. Germany

Library of Congress Cataloging in Publication Data:
Rafoth, Richard, 1945 —
Bicycling Fuel, Nutrition for bicycle riders
Bibliography: p. Includes index
1. Nutrition, handbooks, manuals etc.
2. Bicycles and bicycling, handbooks, manuals etc.
Authorship — handbooks, manuals, etc.
I. Title

Library of Congress Catalog Card Number 88-70209

ISBN 0-933201-17-6 Paperback

About the Author

Richard Rafoth MD is a specialist in diseases of the digestive tract (gastroenterology) and practices in Everett, Washington. Among his hobbies are outdoor physical activities, including cross-country skiing, long distance running, and bicycling.

While preparing with a group of cyclists for the Seattle to Portland Bicycle Classic, a two-hundred mile ride held each June, the issue of nutrition was a frequent topic of discussion during group training rides. Noting the variety of approaches to nutritional conditioning and the many misconceptions, he began to search for a book containing the appropriate facts to set the group straight.

The idea for the present book was born when he failed to find an existing text that was both medically correct and practically oriented. Dr. Rafoth hopes this book will strike the balance between basic physiologic principles and practical application of sound nutritional principles when preparing for and participating in bicycling events.

Table of Contents

Preface

It has been said that some cyclists only bike to eat, while others, who are more competitive, eat to bike. As in most things, the majority of us fall somewhere between these two extremes. Nonetheless, it is a rare outing — be it a training ride, a competitive event, or an afternoon of pleasant spinning — that the topic of food fails to come up. It is my hope that this book will be helpful to everyone with questions about nutrition and cycling, whether they relate to the basic physiology, the mystique of training diets, or how to put together an elegant picnic to complement that crisp day in the country. Enjoy!

1
Basic Physiology

Aside from being a pleasant diversion for the cyclist, food is a necessity that provides the energy required to move man and machine. In this opening section we will discuss the principles of digestion, absorption, and metabolism as they relate to the conversion of food energy into a form that can be used by the muscle cells. When appropriate, the physiology of exercise will be discussed, emphasizing those points that are of particular importance to the bicyclist.

All foods are composed of carbohydrates, fats, and protein. Carbohydrates are the primary energy source for the average recreational cyclist and athletes involved in short, maximum performance events. Fats, which can also serve as an energy source, assume more importance in endurance events. Proteins are used primarily as building blocks to maintain and repair cells throughout the body.

The mechanical energy needed to propel the cyclist over a given distance is a function of both the distance ridden and the energy expended per mile. Since the human 'machine' is not 100% efficient in converting food energy into mechanical energy, the replacement energy requirements, measured in Calories, are equivalent to the mechanical energy expended, divided by the efficiency. It is this energy equivalent that has to be supplied by the food you eat.

The Raw Materials

The energy present in food is released through a chemical reaction with oxygen in a process called oxidation. When this occurs outside the body— for example the burning of oil (a fat) in a lamp or the use of a flaming sugar cube (a carbohydrate) used as a decoration on a dessert — this energy is released in the form of heat and light. In the body, however, food energy needs to be released more slowly and in a form that can be harnessed for basic cell functions as well as transformed into mechanical movement by the muscle cells.

This is accomplished by 'refining' the three basic food materials into a common chemical compound, called adenosine triphosphate, or ATP. It is ATP, produced through the metabolism of the fats, carbohydrates, and protein in our diet, that transfers the food energy to the muscles to meet their energy requirements.

The energy content of equal weights of carbohydrate, fat, and protein varies. It is measured in Calories, in the English system of units, or kilojoules, in the international system of units — see Appendix B for an explanation and the relevant conversion factors. The energy in one nutritional Calorie (spelled with an uppercase C) is the equivalent of a thousand scientific calories (lower case c) or 4.18 kilojoules. As shown in Table 1.1, carbohydrates and protein both contain 4.1 Calories per gram (120 Calories/ounce), while fat contains about twice as many for the same weight. The customary abbreviations for the various units discussed here are as follows:

Calorie: Cal
kilocalorie: kcal
calorie: cal
joule: J
kilojoule: kJ

Digestion

Digestion is the physical and chemical alteration of food so that it can be absorbed into the body by the cells of the intestinal tract. The mechanical and chemical changes occur equally in the stomach and the small intestine, but essentially all absorption takes place in the small intestine.

Now let's take a look at the digestive process with particular attention to those aspects that are important to the cyclist. Figure 1.1, which schematically represents the digestive tract, may be helpful as a reference.

The first step in digestion is mechanical disruption, which allows digestive enzymes to reach the individual food molecules and begin the chemical changes that are required for absorption by the small intestinal cells. This process begins with chewing and continues with the muscular churning of the stomach. It is here that most of the mechanical modification takes place. The mechanical transformation is completed as the semi-liquid material, called *chyme,* proceeds through the small intestine, which comprises the ileum, the duodenum and the jejunum shown in the illustration.

The next step is the chemical processing of the larger food molecules by the digestive enzymes secreted into the chyme by the stomach, pancreas, and small intestinal cells. It is only then that absorption by the small intestinal lining cells can take place.

The time needed by the stomach to complete its work and empty its contents into the small intestine is influenced by several factors. The speed with which this occurs has a direct effect on the time delay

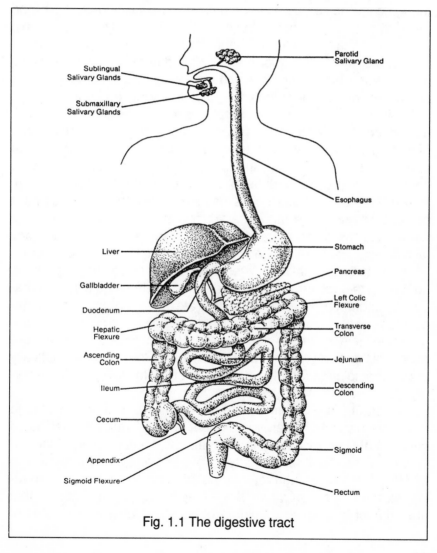

Fig. 1.1 The digestive tract

between eating a food and its availability to the muscle as ATP. The cyclist has direct control over four of these factors:

1. the relative solid/liquid nature of the food;
2. the fat content of the food;
3. the concentration of sugar in the food;
4. the physical activity level of the cyclist.

The more liquid a food, the faster it is emptied from the stomach. Although chewing can be of some help, it is the initial form of the food — liquid or solid — that is most important. Physiologic studies have shown that it takes up to four hours for a solid meal to be mechanically altered into a liquid form and emptied from the stomach, while a meal that is already in the liquid form when it is consumed will be completely emptied into the small intestine within an hour.[31]

Fat in food slows down the emptying of the stomach. As a result, a solid food with a moderate fat content empties slower than a lean or non-fatty one. Likewise, fatty liquids empty more slowly than those that are fat-free. However, the latter still empty faster than low-fat solid food, which must first be mechanically altered by the stomach.

The sugar content of a food is the third factor over which the cyclist has some control. The same characteristics of the small intestine that allow food molecules to pass from the intestinal tract into the body also allow water from the body to be drawn in the opposite direction back into the intestinal tract when a concentrated solution is present. To protect the body from rapid fluid shifts and the resulting dehydration, the stomach slows the emptying rate of very concentrated sugar solutions into the small intestine. The concentration of sugar molecules in solution is referred to as its osmotic activity. The more molecules are present in a given volume, the more 'osmotically active' the solution, and the greater its effect to slow gastric emptying.

This can be a problem for the competitive athlete who wants to maximize his or her energy intake but doesn't want the associated volumes of fluid necessary to maintain the concentration at the optimum for the most rapid emptying of the stomach. The answer to this dilemma lies in the fact that the stomach interprets concentration as the *number of molecules* — regardless of their size — that are present in a specific volume of liquid. If several molecules of sugar (glucose) are linked together, a single complex carbohydrate molecule results that contains the energy equivalent of the several original glucose molecules but is sensed by the stomach as a single molecule. The stomach then senses each complex as a single molecule. Thus, by using complex carbohydrates, the equivalent of more molecules of glucose can be delivered to the small intestine with a given volume of fluid than is possible when only a simple glucose solution is taken.

Finally, the mechanical activity throughout the entire digestive tract is slowed by vigorous physical work or exercise. A fast walk resulting in a heart rate of 108 beats/min was shown to decrease stomach emptying and intestinal absorption by almost 40% in one study.[16] In another, it was demonstrated that above 70% of a person's functional capacity (V_{O2max}), there is a steady slowing until stomach muscular activity stops and no emptying occurs.[6] Fortunately, except for competitive events, cycling does not require a level of exertion that results in this more dramatic effect on the intestinal tract.

Once the cyclist understands how these factors affect stomach emptying, decisions on snacks can be made based on the type of ride that is planned and the anticipated urgency of the caloric replacement. When a *quick* energy boost is needed during the ride, a semi-liquid to liquid simple carbohydrate with minimal fat content is ideal. However, a steady intake is needed as the stomach rapidly empties and the body is once again dependent on its own energy reserves. The endurance rider, on the other hand, might prefer a complex carbohydrate in a more solid form. A small amount of fat is also helpful in prolonging the digestive and absorptive process, providing extra Calories (since fats contain about twice as many Calories per gram as carbohydrates do) and improving the taste.

Carbohydrates

Carbohydrates are the major dietary energy source for most adults, providing anywhere from 40—60% of our daily energy requirements. During exercise the metabolism of the muscle cells shifts and carbohydrates become even more important as the primary fuel source. For that reason, an understanding of their absorption and metabolism is essential in developing a program to maximize performance.

The basic building blocks of all carbohydrates are single sugar molecules, or *monosaccharides*. Glucose and fructose are the two most common monosaccharides in our diet. The linking of two monosaccharides results in a *disaccharide*, while long chains of sugar molecules are referred to as complex carbohydrates, or *polysaccharides*.

Most of our dietary carbohydrate comes from the disaccharides sucrose, or cane sugar, and lactose, or milk sugar, and from complex carbohydrates, called starches, primarily supplied by grains. Before they can be absorbed from the intestinal tract, all disaccharides and complex carbohydrates must first be converted back to the monosaccharide, or single molecule, form.

Digestion of complex carbohydrates begins in the stomach, where salivary enzymes, mixed with food during chewing, convert up to 40% of dietary starch into disaccharide form. The remainder is broken down in the upper small intestine by pancreatic enzymes. The final step in this process, the reduction to monosaccharides, is the result of enzymes secreted by the lining cells of the small intestine.

After monosaccharides are absorbed from the small intestine, they are transported throughout the body via the circulatory system. After absorption into the cell, they can either be metabolized immediately with the release of energy, or stored in the form of glycogen. This is a large polymer of numerous glucose molecules (really just another example of a complex carbohydrate as discussed in the preceding section). Liver and muscle cells are the major storage sites for glycogen. The average 160 pound person has approximately 365 grams of carbohydrate, stored as follows:

liver glycogen:	110 grams
muscle glycogen:	245 grams
extracellular blood sugar:	10 grams

These 365 grams represent almost 1500 Calories of energy, which is available for several hours of cycling at a brisk pace or one hour of out-and-out racing.

Almost all movement of glucose from the blood stream, through the cell wall membrane and into the cells, is controlled by the hormone insulin, which is produced by specialized cells in the pancreas. Although some glucose can enter the cell without insulin, the rate of this transfer increases 25 times when insulin is present. In fact, without insulin the rate of movement into the cell is so slow that there would not be enough energy available to meet the minimal cell energy requirements to sustain life.

Vigorous physical exercise also promotes the movement of glucose into the muscle cell by increasing the permeability of the cell membrane to glucose and by increasing the sensitivity to insulin. During exercise, blood insulin levels have been shown to drop to 50% of their resting level. Although this is not a major factor in normal daily activities, it is important for the athlete.

Insulin is released by the pancreatic cells when they detect a rise in the blood sugar (glucose) level from intestinal absorption. This in turn leads to an increased movement of glucose from the blood stream into the body cells, thus preventing an excessive rise in the blood sugar level. Any excess glucose beyond that needed for immediate cell energy requirements is stored as glycogen.

An understanding of this relationship between food absorption, insulin release, and glucose uptake by the cells is important in planning pre-event nutrition for athletes. If a small amount of glucose in an easily absorbed form, such as a sugar drink, is ingested, it will be emptied quickly from the stomach and absorbed by the intestinal tract. This is followed by a sudden rise in the blood sugar level and an appropriate release of insulin by the pancreatic cells. However, with a pure sugar solution — containing nothing but sucrose and water — the duration of the insulin effect can persist beyond the availability of further glucose from intestinal absorption. The resulting drop in blood sugar level is accentuated by exercise, which also promotes the movement of glucose into the cells.

If the blood sugar drops below a critical level, it is referred to as exercise-induced hypoglycemia and is accompanied by weakness and poor athletic performance. This is accentuated by exercise,which also aids the movement of glucose into the cells. To prevent this form of hypoglycemia, the cyclist should avoid eating or drinking high glucose foods or liquids for at least one hour prior to exercising. The other alternative is to eat only solid complex carbohydrates, which are emptied from the stomach and absorbed more slowly, thereby moderating any swings in blood sugar levels.

During exercise, on the other hand, sugar solutions do not have a negative effect on performance. Exercise increases the movement of blood sugar into the cell, blunting the rise in the blood sugar level from intestinal absorption; insulin release is prevented or minimized; and the overcorrection of the blood sugar level with a drop to hypoglycemic levels does not occur.

Most glucose is metabolized through oxygen-dependent, or *aerobic*, biochemical processes. These are very efficient, with 39% of the energy contained in the glucose molecule being available to the cell via ATP for specific cell functions (the remainder is lost as heat). If the circulatory system is unable to meet the oxygen demands of the muscles during strenuous exercise, oxygen-independent, or *anaerobic*, metabolism occurs. Anaerobic metabolism is not only less efficient, with only 2% of the food energy being made available to the cells, but also leads to the formation of lactic acid, which has additional negative effects on muscle performance.

Fats

Fats provide 20—40% of the Calories in the average American diet. About 95% of dietary fat is in the form of triglycerides, which are composed of a glycerol molecule and three fatty acid (FA) molecules. The

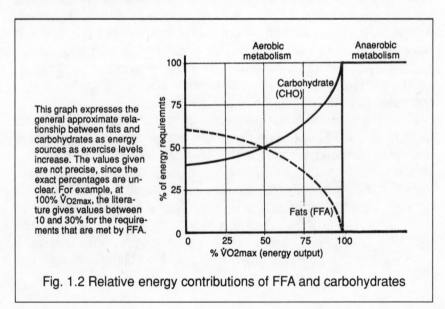

This graph expresses the general approximate relationship between fats and carbohydrates as energy sources as exercise levels increase. The values given are not precise, since the exact percentages are unclear. For example, at 100% $\dot{V}O_2max$, the literature gives values between 10 and 30% for the requirements that are met by FFA.

Fig. 1.2 Relative energy contributions of FFA and carbohydrates

other 5% is cholesterol and phospholipids. While cholesterol and phospholipids are essential building blocks for cell growth, the triglycerides are used primarily as an energy source. They are very important to the endurance cyclist, but play only a minor role in short distance, maximum performance events.

Essentially all fat digestion occurs in the small intestine, with bile from the liver aiding enzymes from the pancreas. The individual fatty acid molecules, which are initially cleaved from the glycerol backbone to become free fatty acids, or FFA for short, are then absorbed by the cells lining the small intestine, move into the lymph system, and are ultimately emptied into the circulatory system. They are then distributed throughout the body and diffuse through the cell membranes, either to be metabolized as an immediate energy source or to be stored after reconstitution to the triglyceride form. Any excess dietary carbohydrate beyond the body's immediate energy needs may also be converted into triglycerides for storage after the body's glycogen stores have been completely filled.

As energy demands increase, the reverse process occurs: triglycerides are broken down into individual fatty acids (FFA), transported to the cells where they are needed, and used as an energy source. As this takes place after all the glycogen stores have been depleted, it is especially important in endurance athletic events.

Protein

Protein is the third major food component and provides approximately 20% of our daily caloric intake. Its major role is to provide the building blocks for cell formation and repair. Detailed studies have shown that the oxidation of protein provides less than 5% of the energy expended during exercise, and it appears that only during starvation or extreme malnutrition is it used as an energy source for normal cell functions.[50, 52]

The building blocks of all protein are the single molecule components called amino acids. Protein digestion begins in the stomach with enzymes secreted by the stomach lining cells and is completed in the small intestine by pancreas and small intestinal cell enzymes. Once digestion has reached the level of free amino acids, they are absorbed by the small intestinal lining cells, transported by the blood, and are rapidly removed by the individual body cells.

Each individual cell has an upper limit to the amount of protein it can store. When this limit is reached, excess amino acids are degraded and transformed into fat or glycogen for storage. As a result, a high protein intake does not automatically result in additional muscle (cell) formation but instead is converted to fat after this critical limit is reached. Studies with athletes have indicated that 1.2 grams of protein per kg body weight per day are adequate for muscle development in most sports, and even in strength training any proteins in excess of 2 g/kg/day will be turned into fat.

The Muscle

The initial sections of this chapter have focused on the three basic food types available to the cyclist as a source of energy, and have emphasized those metabolic characteristics that are unique to each and could impact their use in a high performance dietary program. Now it is time to look at the 'engine' that converts this energy into mechanical performance: the cyclist's muscles.

Skeletal muscle makes up over $1/2$ of the body weight in a lean individual. The muscle cells contain two proteins — actin and myosin — which chemically interact to shorten the muscle fiber when stimulated by nerve impulses. This process requires energy which is provided by ATP

There are two types of muscle fibers. They are referred to as Type I, or slow twitch, and Type II, or fast twitch, fibers. The slow twitch muscle fibers are more efficient in that they use both fats and carbohydrate for energy supply, as shown below. They are the major muscle fiber in use at 70—80% of $\dot{V}_{O2max}$. The fast twitch fibers, on the other hand, are less efficient, using mainly glycogen as fuel. They are called into action for sprints or as the athlete approaches 100% of maximum performance.[23]

The carbohydrates and fats used as fuel by the muscle cells can be provided from reserves within the cell itself (glycogen, triglycerides) or be transported to the cell in the blood stream (glucose, free fatty acids) directly from intestinal absorption or after mobilization from storage elsewhere in the body (liver cells and fatty or adipose tissue). Inside the muscle cell, these basic food components are metabolized to form ATP which then powers the cellular machinery. The muscle cells contain a significant proportion of the body's glycogen stores as well as a small amount of triglycerides. Muscle glygogen and triglycerides offer the advantage of being immediately accessible as an energy source without the intermediate step of transportation by the circulatory system.

Oxygen Consumption

As mentioned previously, the production of ATP is most efficient when adequate oxygen is available for the aerobic metabolism. Oxygen consumption, in formula form expressed as $\dot{V}_{O2}$, is a measurement of the amount of oxygen that is utilized for oxidation and energy production during a specified period of time. Maximum oxygen consumption, referred to as $\dot{V}_{O2max}$, reflects an individual's functional upper limit of aerobic metabolism. At greater levels of exertion, the energy or metabolic requirements of the cells outstrip the ability of the cardiovascular system to deliver the required oxygen and oxygen-independent, or anaerobic, energy production begins.

$\dot{V}_{O2max}$ is dependent on several factors, including lung capacity, heart rate, and the ability of the muscle to extract oxygen from the blood. However, a rough estimate of the level of activity as a percent of $\dot{V}_{O2max}$ can be made from the heart rate alone. If the maximum heart rate (MHR) is considered as 220 — age in years, then 60—70% MHR =50—85% $\dot{V}_{O2max}$.[42] Training tends to increase an

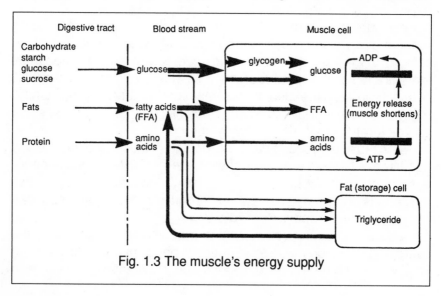

Fig. 1.3 The muscle's energy supply

individual's $\dot{V}_{O2max}$. This is a result of several factors, including an increase in the size and the number of muscle cell mitochondria, an increase in the activity of metabolic enzymes in the muscle cell, an increase in the number of capillaries that supply blood to the muscle, and an increase in the amount of blood the heart can pump (cardiac output).

Anaerobic metabolism occurs during particularly strenuous periods of activity. This process is not only less efficient, with a more rapid depletion of the muscle glycogen stores, but also results in the production of lactic acid as a by-product. It is the build-up of lactic acid and other acid metabolites that ultimately limits performance, even though adequate glycogen stores may remain. The degradation of lactic acid after oxygen becomes available again is responsible for the oxygen debt or recovery phase following anaerobic exercise.

Muscle Energy Supply and Fatigue

Although carbohydrates are the major energy source for the muscles during vigorous activity, fats (via FFA metabolism) can also be an important energy source for the working muscle under aerobic conditions. In fact, it is thought that a shift towards fat metabolism maybe the physiologic explanation for the 'second wind' that can occur with exercise.

Fats can provide over 50% of the Calories expended during moderate exercise, even when adequate glycogen stores are available. As $\dot{V}_{O2max}$ is approached, and anaerobic metabolism becomes more of a factor, their contribution diminishes to between 10 and 30% of total Calories expended. In maximum performance events, where muscle metabolism is entirely anaerobic, fat metabolism ceases and carbohydrates are the only energy source.[2]

When muscle glycogen has been depleted and no additional blood sugar is available as an energy source, the muscle becomes dependent entirely on FFAs for its energy supply. However, since fat is less efficient as an energy source than carbohydrate, energy output can not be maintained above 60—70% $\dot{V}_{O2max}$.[35, 30] It is at this time that fatigue, or the 'bonk,' occurs. If sugar supplements are given, the cyclist will get a boost with an increase in performance until a second limit, which can be referred to as exhaustion, is reached. Even with adequate blood sugar, he or she then has to slow down or stop.[35] Thus there are two levels of fatigue — the first relates to a lack of glucose fuel, and the second relates to changes in the muscle cells themselves.

There are several practical points for the cyclist in this physiology. The first one is that muscle glycogen supports the initial phase of exercise (3—4 hours at 70% $\dot{V}_{O2max}$), while good training as well as riding at a reasonable pace prolong the time of exertion until glycogen is depleted and fatigue occurs. The second point is that maintaining an adequate blood sugar level provides a second source of glucose fuel; this is the reason that a good oral intake of carbohydrates is essential once the muscle glycogen is gone. The third is the fact that even with optimal nutrition, a point is reached where exhaustion occurs and the rider has to slow down or stop.[35, 6] And finally, even though the amount of glycogen in the cell prior to any activity can prolong the duration of that activity to the point of fatigue, it can not increase the muscle's maximum energy output.

Training has two beneficial effects on the relative contribution of carbohydrates and fat as fuel. First, the percentage of Calories derived from fat metabolism at any given activity level is increased with conditioning. [2, 27] The second requires an understanding of the terms *absolute work* and *relative work rate*. Absolute work is the actual number of Calories required to perform any specific task and is the same for all individuals. The relative work rate is dependent on conditioning and indicates what percentage of a person's V_{O2max} is required to perform the task.[23]

With conditioning, any absolute amount of work requires a lesser relative work rate. Referring to Fig. 1.2, it is evident that more Calories will then come from fat metabolism and less from carbohydrate. As a result, the well trained individual will be able to perform at any given level of activity (a certain cycling speed, for example) for a longer time before his or her glycogen reserves are depleted (i.e. before the bonk occurs) and will have more glycogen reserves for a sprint at the end of the race than a less trained competitor.

Muscle glycogen stores are affected by diet. On a high carbohydrate diet the muscle glycogen content is higher than on a low carbohydrate diet of equal caloric value. It has also been shown that if the muscle glycogen stores are completely depleted by exercise, there is an overcompensation when they are replaced — a rebound phenomena. These two observations led to the concept of carbohydrate loading. At its simplest, this refers to a high carbohydrate diet for two or three days immediately prior to an event.

A more extensive carbohydrate loading program adds a preliminary depletion phase, consisting of intensive exercise and two or three days of a low carbohydrate diet prior to the two or three days of high carbohydrate intake. This results in the maximum depletion of muscle glycogen stores and takes advantage of the rebound phenomena during the period of high carbohydrate consumption. The result of this combined program is a muscle glycogen level 50% higher than that on a standard diet.

As with any other motor or engine, the efficiency of the human muscle is calculated as the percentage of the energy input that is converted to actual mechanical work. Under optimal conditions, the muscle converts 20 to 25% of the chemical energy available in the foods we eat into physical performance. The rest is released as heat.

Now that we've covered the major steps in the conversion of the potential energy of food into mechanical work in the muscle, let's review the process as it relates to the typical cycling situation. During prolonged aerobic performance at greater than 50% maximum oxygen uptake (but less than the 100% of maximum performance where anaerobic metabolism comes into play), three distinct phases of muscle metabolism take place.

During the first few minutes, before increased muscle blood flow and hormonal adaptations to exercise have occurred, glycogen is the primary fuel. As much as 20% of the total muscle glycogen stores can be consumed during this phase.

During the second phase, there is a shift in metabolism to a mix of carbohydrate and FFA. Muscle glycogen stores continue to decrease, reflecting their ongoing utilization, but now the muscles also extract and metabolize FFA from the arterial blood supply. During moderate exercise, FFAs and carbohydrates contribute equally as an energy source, while at lesser intensities the ratio changes, with FFAs taking on increasing importance. And, as mentioned above, the percentage of FFAs used at any intensity of exercise increases with training.

The third phase begins when muscle glycogen is completely depleted. It is at this point that a sense of fatigue occurs, exercise intensity can not be maintained, and muscle metabolism shifts almost entirely to FFAs.

Energy Requirements of Cycling

Now that we've reviewed the process of converting food energy into the mechanical activity of the muscles, let's look at the energy requirements of cycling. This will help in planning an appropriate nutrition program.

As we discuss the energy requirements of bicycling, reference will again be made to the terms Calorie and calorie. Here it should be pointed out that these terms can not only be used to express the energy content of different foods, but also the energy released by cellular metabolism and the mechanical or other physical work actually performed.

In physical science, the calorie is defined as the quantity of heat required to raise the temperature of 1 gram of water 1 degree centigrade. As this unit is too small to easily express the energy utilized and expended in biologic systems, the Calorie, which is equivalent to 1000 calories (or 1 kcal), is used in discussions of human energy metabolism.

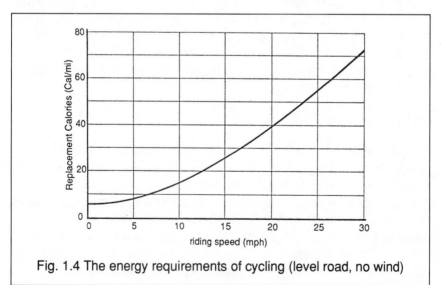

Fig. 1.4 The energy requirements of cycling (level road, no wind)

In the previous sections we have emphasized that ATP, or adenosine triphosphate, is the common energy carrier which transfers the potential energy in foodstuffs to the cells. As this energy transfer takes place, large portions are lost as heat. On the average, about 60 percent of all the energy in the food we eat becomes heat during the process of ATP formation. Still more energy is lost as heat when energy transfer takes place from ATP to the functional systems of the cell, including muscle contraction. The result is that no more than 25 percent of all the energy in food is actually available for mechanical work performance by the muscles.

The bicycle itself is a very efficient machine. Over 95% of the energy expended by the cyclist is translated into forward motion and less than 5% is lost as heat due to the resistance of the bearings, rolling resistance of the tires, etc.[47]

On a level surface, aerodynamic drag, or wind resistance, consumes most of the cyclist's energy output. This aerodynamic resistance is a function of the cyclist's speed relative to the mass of air through which the bicycle is moving — not relative to the ground. That is why a headwind will increase energy needs for a given ground speed, and a tailwind will decrease them.

The relationship between energy requirements and air speed is an exponential one. This means that doubling the forward speed more than doubles the energy requirements. The actual relationship is illustrated in Fig. 1.2 and Table 1.3. If the terrain is not level, additional energy will be required to raise bike and rider against gravity. The specifics of this calculation are covered in Appendix A. To give some perspective, the energy expenditure per mile of cycling is about one fifth of that of running.

Bicycling and Weight Control

A natural extension to any discussion of aerobic exercise and energy utilization is the role of that activity in a weight control program. Physical activity has a positive effect on a weight loss regimen through appetite suppression, increased energy expenditure, and the maintenance of lean muscle tissue at the expense of fat. The basic premise of all weight control programs is that the number of Calories being expended by the body should be greater than the number of Calories consumed, resulting in an overall net deficit. This deficit is then covered by Calories derived from the body's fat reserves, resulting in weight loss.

One interesting aspect is the unavoidable weight loss that occurs in some competitive athletes no matter how many Calories they attempt to eat. When examined closely, it was found that this was another example of the Calories expended being more than the number eaten. This phenomenon was most pronounced in competitive swimmers. As a group, they would train long hours, were unable to eat while swimming, and then had too few waking hours left to replace the needed Calories (as many as 7000 Calories with only 6 or 7 non-exercise waking hour).[49] Because cyclists can eat while riding, this is not a major problem for this group.

Many dieters claim that vigorous activity actually increases appetite, and several early population studies appeared to support the idea that appetite was regulated by exercise in such a way as to maintain a constant body weight. The assumption was that any weight loss benefits of exercise would be limited unless the individual had extreme self control. However, recent, more carefully controlled studies of overweight individuals have proven that additional physical activity does not stimulate a proportionate increase in appetite and is helpful in achieving a net negative caloric balance and weight loss.

An additional benefit of vigorous exercise is the suppression of appetite that occurs immediately afterwards and lasts for several hours. This short term effect can be used as an appetite control strategy by planning an exercise period immediately prior to the major meal of the day.

Bicycling, or any other exercise program, increases an individual's caloric expenditures in several ways. First, and most significant, is the immediate energy requirement of the working muscles to move bicycle and rider against the resistance of the air and gravity. The number of Calories consumed is a function of the weight of the bicycle and its rider, the speed at which they are moving, and the duration of the ride. An additional, indirect, effect is that individuals in an exercise program report an increased vigor and sense of wellbeing, often changing other aspects of their daily routine to include more physical activity — for example routinely walking up a flight of stairs instead of taking the elevator.

One unconfirmed study recently suggested that there was an advantage to cycling in a weight loss program. The dieters were divided in three exercise groups — swimmers, walkers, and cyclists. For an equivalent exercise level, the cyclists lost most weight.[19] It will be interesting to see if these results can be duplicated.

Exercise also has a beneficial effect on the basal metabolic rate, or BMR. This is the number of Calories being utilized when the body is at rest to maintain the basic life processes. Recent studies have demonstrated that a regular exercise program not only prevents the usual slowing of this basal rate associated with dietary restriction, which is a natural adaptive response to starvation that prolongs survival, but have also hinted at an increase in the BMR compared to that on a normal diet without exercise. These effects on the BMR are associated with any aerobic conditioning activity and can be maintained with 30 to 40 minutes of vigorous exercise 3 or 4 times a week.

A final benefit of physical activity relates to the protection of lean body tissue during periods of caloric restriction and weight loss. This results in the preferential loss of body fat and preservation of muscle when a negative caloric balance exists.

Both as a measure of their efficiency as energy sources, and as a measure of their respective impact on a weight control program, Table 1.1 compares the number of Calories supplied to the body by carbohydrates, fats and protein, respectively.

Although the bottom line of any cycling weight control program will be read from the bathroom scale, a rough estimate can be made using the caloric expenditure for cycling, as summarized in Table 1.3., the number of Calories consumed, and the fact that a pound of body fat (455 grams) contains approximately 3500 Calories. This relationship is expressed in the following formula:

$$W = (C_i - C_b - C_e) / 3500$$

where:

$W =$	weight gain or loss in pounds
$C_i =$	Calories ingested
$C_b =$	basal metabolic rate
$C_e =$	additional Calories expended through exercise

The basal daily caloric expenditure varies depending on sex, age, and usual activity level, but for purposes of this calculation it can be estimated with sufficient accuracy from Table 1.2.

Table 1.1 Energy contents of carbohydrates, fats, and proteins

Food type	Energy content	
	Cal/g	(kJ/g)
carbohydrates (both starch and sugars)	4.1	(17.2)
fats (both dietary fat and body fat)	9.3	(38.9)
protein	4.1	(17.2)

Table 1.2. Bicycling and weight control

C_i = Calories eaten per 24 hours ....

C_b = Basal metabolic rate (BMR — see below) ....

C_e = Calories expended by cycling (see Table 1.3) ....

C_l = caloric balance = $C_i - C_b - C_e$ ....

Weight gain or loss in pounds = C_l / 3500 = ...

C_b (BMR) for 165 lbs (70 kg) person:

1. Base rate Calories: ....
(men: weight in pounds x 0.45
women: weight in pounds x 0.40)

2. Activity level Calories: ....
(sedentary: 0.2 x base rate
light activity: 0.3 x base rate
moderate activity: 0.4 x base rate
heavy work: 0.5 x base rate)

3. Metabolic needs of eating: ....
(0.1 x base rate Calories)

Cb (BMR): 1 + 2 + 3 = ...

Table 1.3 Calories required as a function of speed, time, and distance

Riding speed		Replacement Calories			
mph	(km/h)	Cal/mile	(Cal/km)	Cal/hr	(Cal/min)
5	(8.0)	7.4	(4.6)	87	(1.5)
6	(9.6)	8.3	(5.2)	100	(1.7)
7	(11.2)	9.3	(5.8)	115	(1.9)
8	(12.8)	10.5	(6.6)	134	(2.2)
9	(14.4)	11.9	(7.4)	157	(2.6)
10	(16.0)	13.4	(8.4)	184	(3.1)
11	(17.6)	15.1	(9.4)	216	(3.6)
12	(19.2)	16.9	(10.6)	253	(4.2)
13	(20.8)	18.9	(11.8)	296	(4.9)
14	(22.4)	21.1	(13.2)	345	(5.7)
15	(24.0)	23.4	(14.6)	401	(6.7)
16	(25.6)	25.8	(16.2)	463	(7.7)
17	(27.2)	28.5	(17.8)	534	(8.9)
18	(28.8)	31.3	(19.5)	613	(10.2)
19	(30.4)	34.2	(21.4)	700	(11.7)
20	(32.0)	37.3	(23.3)	797	(13.3)
21	(33.6)	40.6	(25.4)	903	(15.0)
22	(35.2)	44.0	(27.5)	1019	(17.0)
23	(36.7)	47.6	(29.8)	1146	(19.1)
24	(38.4)	51.4	(32.1)	1283	(21.4)
25	(40.0)	55.3	(34.6)	1433	(23.9)
26	(41.6)	59.4	(37.1)	1594	(26.6)
27	(43.2)	63.6	(39.8)	1767	(29.5)
28	(44.8)	68.0	(42.5)	1954	(32.6)
29	(46.4)	72.5	(45.3)	2154	(35.9)
30	(48.0)	77.2	(48.2)	2365	(39.4)

Remarks:

1. Replacement means Calories to be eaten to replace those expended if no change in body weight is planned. These values are based on a 25% efficiency of the human 'machine.'

2. Included is the basal metabolism at 50 Cal/hr.

2
Nutrition Theory

After covering, in the preceding chapter, the basic physiology necessary to understand the nutritional requirements of biking, we shall
now apply these principles to develop a practical nutritional program
that allows us to maximize both performance and enjoyment of the
sport.

As we discuss diet, three activity levels should be considered. First
is that of the recreational rider, who cycles for several hours at no
more than 60—70% of his or her potential. Then there is the activity
level of the endurance athlete, who rides longer distances, usually
100 km (62,5 miles) or more, at the same pace. Finally, there is that
of the competitive cyclist, who performs at more than 70% of his or
her maximum.

General Background

Analyzing the typical American diet reveals that 46% of the Calories
are provided by carbohydrates (16% from free sugars and 30% from
complex carbohydrates); 42% are from fats, and 12% from protein.
Over the last 50 years there has been an increase in fats from 32%
to 42%, at the expense of complex carbohydrates, which have
declined from 40% to 30% over this period.[46]

The primary role of carbohydrates, contained mainly in fruits,
vegetables, and grains, is as a source of energy for the human power
plant. By providing this fuel, they spare stored fats and, more impor-
tantly, cellular proteins that would otherwise be broken down and metabolized for their energy content. Aside from their value as an energy
source, carbohydrates are not essential for any specific metabolic
function.

Recent studies have focused on the particular type of carbohydrate in the diet, comparing the relative effects of simple carbohydrates, such as refined sugar, to those of complex carbohydrates,
i.e. starches. Increasingly, evidence supports the advantages of
complex carbohydrates, which are absorbed more slowly, require

less insulin for their metabolism and, as a result, produce a more even and constant blood sugar level

Fats are also an energy source but differ from carbohydrates in that they provide some essential building blocks for the cellular machinery. This means that they cannot be synthesized or produced by the body. These essential fats include certain fatty acids (linoleic acid), as well as cholesterol and phospholipids. It has been estimated that these essential requirements would be met with a diet containing only 15—25 grams of fat (135—225 Calories or about 10% of our total daily caloric needs), while the additional Calories are used only for their energy value.

Studies of the various groups of non-essential dietary fats have repeatedly demonstrated the harmful effects of saturated animal fats as opposed to the benefits of unsaturated vegetable fats and certain fatty acids found in fish oils (eicosapentaenoic acid). These findings, coupled with the evidence that a diet which is high in fat contributes to obesity and heart disease, have resulted in strong recommendations to cut the percentage of our daily Calories provided by fats and to use 'good' fats in food preparation whenever possible. There are limits to these reductions, however, as fat content is important to the texture and taste appeal of the food.

Proteins are the third major constituents of our diet. While fats and carbohydrates are used mainly as an energy source for our daily activities, protein provides the basic building blocks for cell growth and repair. As with fats, there are certain essential amino acids (the building blocks of proteins) which cannot be produced by the body and are mandatory dietary requirements. However, once these needs have been met there is no evidence that additional protein is helpful even to the vigorous athlete. The additional dietary protein required for the muscle growth stimulated by conditioning is quite small when compared to the normal daily intake, and there is no evidence that a high protein diet will speed up or force this muscle development. In fact, there is some evidence that a routinely high protein diet may be harmful to the kidneys.

Ongoing interest and research into the health effects of the American diet will undoubtedly result in further changes in our typical diet. The evidence suggests that these changes will include an overall reduction in fat content, emphasizing the benefits of certain types of fats, with a corresponding increase in the carbohydrate content to make up the resulting Calorie deficit.

Based on the physiologic principles reviewed in Chapter 1, it is easy to identify carbohydrates as the optimum food for all athletic activities. They are easily digested and absorbed, and are also the most readily metabolized to ATP. Fats have the disadvantage of slowing gastric emptying and absorption, while proteins have a very complex metabolism that limits their availability as an energy source.

During exercise, certain glucose stores are used preferentially to meet the energy requirements of the muscle cell. The glucose stored in the muscle fibers as glycogen is used first. Once the muscle glycogen has been depleted, the blood becomes the most important glucose source. As blood glucose (blood sugar) is used, it is replaced by mobilizing glycogen from the liver. Any glucose absorbed from the digestive tract is extracted from the blood by the muscle and helps to conserve the liver glycogen. When the liver glycogen is depleted, the muscle cell is dependent on either absorbed glucose or fat metabolism to meet its energy needs. If there is no glucose available from digestion, hypoglycemia and fatigue occur.[35, 11]

Pre-Exercise Diet

The body's glycogen stores on a normal diet (365 grams, or 1500 Calories — see Chapter 1) will support several hours of submaximal cycling before complete depletion and fatigue occur. Although these are adequate for the average recreational cyclist and for those participating in competitive events lasting less than one hour, the endurance rider and the racer participating in longer events will benefit from pre-exercise carbohydrate loading to maximize muscle glycogen reserves.

The amount of glycogen stored in the muscles is directly related to the carbohydrate content of the diet. After three days on a high-carbohydrate diet (providing at least 70% of the total dietary Calories in the form of carbohydrate), the total muscle glycogen stores are significantly greater than after a standard diet. When the muscle glycogen is depleted by vigorous exercise immediately before beginning a high carbohydrate diet, this difference is accentuated.

The standard carbohydrate loading program is started six days prior to the anticipated competitive event. A vigorous daily workout of one to two hours each of the first three days depletes the muscles' glycogen reserves. During this period, the athlete stays on a low carbohydrate diet (a maximum of 10% of total Calories from carbohydrates) to maximize the effects of exercise. This is followed by three days of a carbohydrate rich diet with only light exercise to maintain muscle flexibility. During these final three days, the cyclist should eat at least 600 grams of carbohydrate per 24 hours. The last carbohydrates are consumed 4 to 6 hours prior to the event.[28, 40]

Some disadvantages of carbohydrate loading include the difficulty of maintaining the initial low carbohydrate diet, problems with weight gain during the high carbohydrate and low exercise portion of the program, and complaints of muscle heaviness and stiffness thought to result from the excess glycogen and associated water present in the muscle fibers.

The amount of water retention is not insignificant. For each gram of carbohydrate stored, 3 grams of water are stored as well. This equals a 2 to 7 pound weight gain from water alone.[52] This water retension is not all bad in that, as the glycogen is utilized during exercise, the water is released and will help cut down fluid replacement needs. Although there have been additional concerns about EGK (cardiac) changes due to glycogen loading of the heart muscle, as well as possible long term harmful effects, these have not been substantiated.[3]

Even though muscle glycogen is predictably increased with this program, it is not clear that performance is enhanced more than with a 3-day high carbohydrate diet alone, i.e. without the initial depletion phase.[40] An explanation may lie in the results of one study which indicated that trained endurance athletes achieved the maximum possible muscle glycogen stores with rest and a high carbohydrate diet alone.[6] Considering the many potential problems and the questionable benefit of the full six-day program, most athletic trainers currently recommend three days of high carbohydrate intake immediately prior to the event and eliminate the depletion phase.

Although carbohydrates are beneficial in the pre-exercise program, there is one critical period when their intake should be limited. This is the several hours immediately prior to exercise. With the insulin surge that follows the absorption of carbohydrates, the additive effect of exercise to facilitate the movement of glucose into the cell, and the possibility of hypoglycemia, a poor performance can result. Therefore it is currently recommended that only complex carbohydrates — not simple sugars — be taken, and then at least an hour before exercise.

A second issue is the tendency of nervousness to delay gastric emptying. Because of the stomach distention that can develop, some authorities suggest that any nutrition be taken at least three hours before the event, and that it be in the liquid form and low in fat content to minimize this risk.

There is a consensus, however, on the importance of the pre-race meal. While it takes up to two days to replace muscle glycogen stores, liver glycogen is much more easily modified by diet. The pre-race meal is the key in assuring that these liver glycogen stores are at their maximum.

The best strategy appears to be a light (200 gram) carbohydrate meal, low in fat, four hours before the event, and a 45 gram confectionary bar five minutes before. [6] A survey of competitive cyclists disclosed the following carbohydrate favorites:

vegetables	51%
pancakes	44%
fruits	81%
soft drinks	56%
cereal	50%

There has been very little work on fat and protein requirements in the pre-exercise period, and no suggestion that either is of any specific benefit or harm. One common misconception is that an increase in dietary protein will force muscle development. The only stimulus for muscle growth is resistive training, or conditioning. A normal balanced diet, which contains almost twice the minimum daily protein requirements, provides more than enough excess protein to support the maximum muscle mass increase of one pound per week. In fact, increasing dietary protein may be counterproductive if protein Calories replace carbohydrate in the three-day pre-exercise period. The same is true for fats, which are notorious for their appetite suppressant effect.

A final word of caution is to avoid any major changes in diet during the pre-competition period, unless you have tried similar modifications before. The above suggestions need to be customized for your own digestive and metabolic functions. Any advantage of carbohydrate loading, or shifting the make-up of your diet, can be more than offset by the GI distress or indigestion brought on by new foods or food combinations. As in all things, moderation is important, and a balanced diet with an emphasis on carbohydrates appears to offer the maximum benefits during this period.

Exercise

Early in the exercise period, almost all the glucose fuel for the muscle cell comes from muscle glycogen. As this muscle glycogen is steadily depleted, the percentage of energy supplied from blood glucose steadily increases until it reaches 100% in the third and fourth hour.[35,] [11] Initially, the blood sugar level is maintained by the breakdown and release of liver glycogen. However, at three to four hours it is estimated that three quarters of the glucose metabolized is from oral intake and one quarter from either liver glycogen or gluconeogenesis (i.e. glucose formed as an intermediate step in fat or protein metabolism).[10]

This relationship between muscle, liver, and blood glucose explains the performance enhancing effect of oral carbohydrate feedings on exercise lasting more than one hour. In fact, one study suggested that after only one hour of exercise blood sugar was already supplying 75—90% of the carbohydrate needed for metabolism by the muscles.[6] If oral caloric supplements are started early in the ride, they conserve liver glycogen and delay the time at which complete depletion (fatigue) occurs. Any carbohydrates taken in after liver glycogen has already been exhausted provides an immediate energy boost.

It should be remembered that fats in the form of FFA also supply energy for the active muscle. The fact that fat metabolism provides a greater percentage of the total Calories expended at lower $\dot{V}_{O2}$ presents us with another option to protecting the body's glycogen reserves. Indeed, 'going out fast' at more than 70% of $\dot{V}_{O2max}$ is very inefficient in terms of glycogen use, with almost all the expended Calories coming form muscle and liver glycogen. The more prudent cyclist marshals his resources at 50—70% $\dot{V}_{O2max}$. This spares both muscle and liver glycogen, with preferential use of oral glucose supplements — the reverse of the situation at higher energy levels.[6]

The type of sugar eaten, i.e. glucose versus fructose, does not appear to be a factor one way or another, but the form of the supplement does.[30, 6] One study compared equal caloric feedings of liquid and solid carbohydrates. It was demonstrated that although maximum pace, heart rate, and total energy expenditure were the same, the riders eating the more solid carbohydrated were able to sustain a longer sprint to exhaustion at the end of the ride.[9] It can be speculated that this relates to a more sustained release of energy as the body takes additional time to digest and absorb the solid carbohydrate.[1]

Hence, solid carbohydrate appears to be the preferable replacement to start within the first hour of the ride. On the other hand, when a quick energy boost is needed after all glycogen reserves have been exhausted, it seems logical that a liquid glucose drink would be optimal. This minimizes the delay in stomach emptying and absorption time, although frequent drinks are required to maintain these benefits.

Recently glucose polymers, complex molecules made up of individual glucose molecules, have been developed and are marketed both as a powder and as ready-mixed sports drinks. These appear to combine the beneficial characteristics of both forms: they are readily absorbed due to their liquid form and provide the prolonged benefits of a more slowly digested and absorbed complex carbohydrate.[24]

Once again, there has been little work on the physiologic effects of fats and protein eaten during the exercise period. Fats improve the taste of snacks and may be helpful in counteracting the natural depression of appetite that occurs with exercise, but delays in stomach emptying may lead to nausea if taken in large amounts. The same is true for proteins, though to a lesser degree.

In 1984, White and his associates analyzed the diet of an ultra-distance cyclist during a 24-hour event.[45] They found that the percentage of total energy derived from proteins (10%) and fats (30%) decreased, with a marked shift towards carbohydrates (60%). This compares with the normal pattern of 15% protein, 40% fat, and 45% carbohydrate. In addition, there was an increase in the intake of liquids, with semisolid (36%) and liquid foods (30%) providing more than half the Calories. This shift appeared to result from the increased fluid needs of exercise as well as from the decreased sensation of abdominal fullness due to the improved gastric emptying and absorption of liquids. Even with these changes, and a strong emphasis on maintaining a good intake during the ride, it was still possible to supply only a little more than half (54%) of the total estimated energy requirements of the event (19,755 Calories).

Post-Exercise Diet

The most common mistake in exercise nutrition is the failure to appreciate the importance of the post-exercise diet. Most athletes feel that after a long training ride or competitive event the only diet issue is when to begin carbohydrate loading for the next session. There are two important benefits of a good post-exercise regimen, and once again both the selection of carbohydrates and the timing of replacement play key roles.

Muscle glycogen depletion is thought to play a role in the stiffness that follows strenuous exercise. It appears that one benefit of vigorous carbohydrate repletion is to minimize this 'day-after effect' of a training ride or competitive event. A second concern is that failure to completely replace the muscle glycogen stores depleted by a regular vigorous training program may account for the stale feeling that occurs after several consecutive days of exercise. Blunting both of these effects of glycogen depletion should be helpful in meeting training goals.

Liver glycogen is restored quickly and easily if a high carbohydrate diet is followed. Complete muscle glycogen replacement, on the other hand, requires 48 hours, although the majority of the replacement is accomplished in the first 24 hours.[6, 8] As in pre-event carbohydrate loading, a daily intake of 600 grams of carbohydrate achieves optimal results, and it appears that complex carbohydrates, i.e. starches, are superior to free glucose in speedily completing the process.[6, 49]

It has been noted that for several hours immediately following vigorous exercise, glucose is taken up by the muscles three times as fast as it is six to twelve hours later.[25] This may be of benefit to someone who is in a daily workout program and needs every possible advantage in replacing muscle glycogen.

Although some muscle breakdown occurs with all vigorous exercise, leading one to speculate about the potential benefits of protein supplements, the normal American diet contains more than enough protein to provide the raw materials for any repairs necessary.

Water

Water is not a source of nutrition for the athlete. Yet adequate hydration is as important to good athletic performance as the type and form of the food eaten, if not more so. Total body fluid losses during exercise result in a decrease in both plasma volume (the fluid circulating within the blood vessels) and muscle water. As this fluid loss progresses, physical performance deteriorates.

A practical assessment of the importance of dehydration on cycling performance was undertaken by White and Ford in 1983.[44] In this study, seven elite cycling endurance performers completed a 103 km course over a $2^1/2$-hour period at an average speed of 41.9 km/hr (26 mph). They found that:

1. body weight losses averaged 3.25%;
2. relatively low volumes of fluid were ingested during the race;
3. little or no fluid intake occurred in two competitors who retired early with symptoms of heat distress.

The results indicated that even medium distance road racing produced significant body weight (fluid) loss. Even more significant was the finding that most of the cyclists involved in the study were unaware of the importance of fluid intake in minimizing the harmful effects of dehydration on performance.

In a second study, an experimental protocol was designed using a windload simulator. Work loads were structured to require approximately 67% of each subject's previously determined maximum aerobic performance ($\dot{V}_{O2max}$). This resulted in an average weight loss of 1.9% at 1 hour and 3.6% at 2 hours if no fluids were ingested. Physiologic measurements were made with no fluid replacement, with complete replacement using water, and with replacement using an electrolyte drink.

Without replacement, there was increasing work intolerance, as indicated by an increase in heart rate and systolic blood pressure. With ongoing replacement, this effect was minimized and there was a more rapid return to the pre-exercise baseline during the recovery period. Aside from a taste preference, there was no apparent benefit to replacement with the electrolyte drink over water alone during the 2-hour trial. However, the fact that relatively large fluid volumes needed to be replaced (2300 ml) indicates that palatability and gastric acceptance of fluids are important considerations in the selection of replacement fluids.

The most outstanding finding was not the effect of dehydration on performance, but how rapidly serious fluid deficiencies could occur with minimal awareness on the part of the athlete. It pointed out that the sensation of thirst lags well behind the body's needs, and emphasized that a successful fluid replacement program should begin at the same time as the ride.

Sports Drinks

Carbohydrate drinks, so called sports drinks, are important if a strenuous ride in excess of two hours is planned. The body's stores of glycogen will support vigorous exercise for approximately two hours before depletion and subsequent fatigue occur. Any carbohydrate ingested and metabolized during this period will spare the body's glycogen reserves. Although it does not increase maximum performance levels, it will prolong the duration of exercise before exhaustion occurs. To put this into perspective, a 10% glucose solution, equivalent to a regular cola or similar soft drink, taken at a rate of a quart per hour would provide 260 Calories per hour. A 165 lb cyclist riding at 15 mph burns 400 Calories/h; at 20 mph 800 Calories/h are required (see Table 1.3). Thus this replacement alone would provide a 25—50% increase in endurance.

While exercise physiologists agree that carbohydrate replacement is of value in prolonged exercise, there is considerable debate as to the merits of carbohydrate polymers versus simple sugars (glucose). Neither David Lamb, at Ohio State's Human Performance Laboratory, nor Mark Davis, at the University of South Carolina, have been able to demonstrate any advantage to glucose polymers over simple sugars in enhancing performance.[51] Likewise, a study by

Quaker Oats found no difference in the enhancement of long distance cycling performance when a 6% sucrose/glucose solution was compared to a 7% glucose polymer/fructose drink.[51]

Although they appear to be physiologically equivalent when equal Calories are provided, the one advantage of polymers is that they are not as sweet as simple sugar drinks. Since sweet tasting drinks discourage fluid replacement, this can be a major advantage of polymer drinks in promoting fluid replacement.

Drugs and Vitamins

Once the basics of nutrition are understood and implemented, it's not unusual to see competitive cyclists begin to investigate other supplements to enhance their performance. Some, such as ephedrine, are banned in sanctioned competitive events and will not be discussed further.

The use of dietary supplements to enhance performance can be traced back at least as far as the Romans, who drank lion's blood purportedly to improve their strength and courage. Today's additives, mainly amino acids and vitamins, are often used with little more proof of benefit than was available to the Romans. In addition to the lack of any controlled scientific studies to support their benefits, the potential side effects as well as the high cost of these supplements need to be considered.

Vitamins are often touted as a safe and effective way of improving performance. Although they are frequently recommended by coaches, and used by competitive athletes, there is no evidence that any athlete on a balanced diet improves his or her performance with vitamin supplements. In addition, there is good evidence that megavitamin programs can be harmful. This is particularly true with the fat-soluble vitamins (A, E, D, and K), which can accumulate in the body and reach toxic levels. But even with the use of water-soluble vitamins (B complex and C), any excess of which is excreted in the urine, there have been reports of harmful side effects at mega-doses (usually 10 to 100 times the recommended daily requirements). If there is a continued concern about how well balanced a diet is, there is no harm (other than to your wallet) in using a simple over-the-counter multiple vitamin once a day 'just to be safe.'

Amino acids are the building blocks of proteins and are present in all foods we eat. As with vitamins, a balanced diet should provide more than enough of all the essential amino acids, and there is no proof (with the possible exception of L-carnitine) that the available supplements enhance performance. The bottle of amino acids sold in the health food store for $20—$30 has no proven benefit over a glass of milk and a peanut butter sandwich, and doesn't have nearly the same taste appeal. In addition, there is growing evidence that excess protein in the diet may place undue additional stress on the kidneys and may be harmful over long periods.

Of the popular supplements, vitamin B_{15} (also known as D_{15} or pangamic acid), octacosanol, trimethylglycine, gamma-oryzanol, and inosine are of unproven benefit. L-carnitine, sodium bicarbonate, and caffeine may be of some use in certain situations and will be discussed further.

L-carnitine is the one amino acid that has been studied in conditioned athletes and may be of benefit. In an Italian study, it was found to promote glycogen sparing (through increased utilization of fatty acids), allowing a longer ride to exhaustion. In addition, there was the suggestion that conditioned athletes could also raise their VO_{2max}.[34] However, these results have not been confirmed by other investigators and the potential side effects of this agent have not yet been completely explored.

Sodium bicarbonate is the second substance that has been studied in a controlled manner and has been demonstrated to improve performance. It is available in the form of baking soda or Alka-Seltzer, and presumably works by neutralizing the lactic acid that builds up in the muscles during exercise. The blood's natural buffering capacity provides this function during sustained exercise, but bicarbonate appears to be of help during short sprints when lactic acid accumulates more quickly. In a study at Iowa State University, cyclists improved their sprinting ability significantly by taking 2 tablespoons of baking soda just prior to the event. However, side effects in the form of diarrhea and stomach upset were common, and it appears to be of use only in short races such as a 4000 meter pursuit.[9, 34]

Caffeine

Finally, no discussion of performance enhancers would be complete without mentioning caffeine. During prolonged (endurance) exercise, the onset of fatigue correlates closely with the depletion of muscle glycogen stores and is delayed if muscle glycogen is spared. The metabolism of free fatty acids as an alternative energy source should result in a decreased use of muscle glycogen during exercise.

Caffeine does increase blood FFA, and in one study produced a 50% increase with a peak at three to four hours.[49] This effect on FFA is seen after a dose of 5mg/kg of body weight, which is the equivalent of 2 cups of coffee (300 mg caffeine) for a 70 kg person.[36] A second possibility is that caffeine works on the central nervous system as a general stimulant and suppressor of intolerance to pain from lactate build-up during anaerobic exercise.[9]

There are negative effects as well. One is the diuretic effect, which leads to frequent urination and results in a net body fluid deficit and dehydration. Others are an increased heart rate and an increase in the athlete's anxiety level. But by far the biggest negative is that caffeine in high concentrations is a drug in the eyes of the US Olympic Committee.

Controversy continues over the practical benefits of caffeine. The original study at Ball State University demonstrated a 20% increase in endurance performance after the equivalent of 3 cups of coffee or 6 caffeinated colas. Subsequent studies have been less convincing. In addition, physiologists believe that caffeine's effects may be negated on race day because of the high adrenaline levels in the body. Nonetheless, the consensus of endurance athletes is that caffeine can be useful if used correctly. This includes a period of abstinence for several weeks before the race, because habitual use induces tolerance.[34]

To put additives in their proper perspective, it should be pointed out that 35% of all subjects have a positive response to any pill, including those without an active ingredient — the placebo response. It is possible that this psychological lift is the major benefit of most performance enhancers. Any improvement in the few controlled studies done thus far has been small, a few per cent at most, and would be of benefit only to the competitive athlete who has already been on an optimum training and nutritional program. The average recreational bicyclist, on the other hand, has little if anything to gain from this group of substances.

Minerals, Trace Elements

Minerals are chemical elements found in the body either in their basic form or complexed with organic molecules. Like vitamins, they are essential for normal cell functioning. The two most prevalent minerals, calcium and phosphorous, are major components of bone, while sodium and potassium are found in all tissue fluids, both within and around the cells. Magnesium, chloride, sulfur, and zinc are other minerals that play a key role in cell function. The trace elements iron, manganese, copper, and iodine are found in much smaller quantities but also play essential roles as catalysts in the chemical processes basic to life.

These minerals, found in all foods, are maintained in balance through regulatory mechanisms for both absorption and excretion. As a result of this close control, they are easily provided by a balanced diet. With the increase in Calories required to meet training needs, the athlete enjoys the additional protection of an increased mineral intake. As a result, mineral deficiencies are extremely rare, even on unusual training diets. Only calcium and iron appear to be required by some athletes in increased amounts. Because of toxic effects when ingested in large amounts, minerals as a group are not recommended as a routine dietary supplement.

This is also true for sodium chloride, or table salt. Over a 24-hour period, the athlete's standard training diet replaces two to three times the normal salt losses. Only under the extreme environmental conditions of very high temperatures or high humidity is a salt supplement needed. An exception may be the cyclist who has not trained for the event and can lose excessive amounts of salt in perspiration.[52, 49, 36] Although exercise cramps were once thought to be a result of salt deficiency, it appears that they are more likely a heat cramp related to dehydration and a decreased blood flow to the muscles.[30]

Calcium metabolism is still not completely understood in the athlete. The question of an increased calcium requirement is tied to concerns about osteoporosis in women athletes who, because of the intensity of their training, have become amenorrheic. The hormonal changes that occur in this situation affect bone formation and are felt to be the cause. On the other hand, recent evidence has suggested that the positive effects of exercise on bone formation may counteract and cancel out the bone loss. At this time, there is no consensus on the need for calcium supplements and the controversy is mentioned here for completeness only.

Iron, on the other hand, has been studied extensively in athletes. A deficiency state does occur with a negative effect on performance. Again, this is more of a problem for the woman athlete, because of the additional iron needs to replace menstrual blood loss. When the US Olympic team was studied, it was found that 20 to 30% of the female athletes did not get adequate iron.[22] As iron can be toxic, any question of a deficiency state is best resolved by a screening blood count and serum iron or ferritin assay before resorting to supplements.

Fiber

Dietary fiber has received considerable attention over the last few years. Fiber is a general term for the indigestible carbohydrate in the diet and refers mainly to the cellulose, lignin, and pectin found in fruits, grains, and vegetables.

Its major function is to provide bulk in the diet to aid in regular elimination. There has been some evidence that population groups with a traditionally low fiber diet also have an increased incidence of diverticulosis, cardiovascular disease, colon cancer and diabetes. The difficulty with these studies is that the ethnic groups that eat a low fiber diet also have a higher percentage of their total dietary Calories provided by fats and refined sugars. Therefore it may be the excess fats, for example, rather than the lack of fiber that is the culprit.

Currently there is no recommended minimum for dietary fiber and no special requirements for cyclists or other athletes. On the other hand, there is evidence that too much fiber may bind minerals such as zinc in the intestinal tract, resulting in poor absorption. The most reasonable approach seems to be a well balanced diet with enough fruits, grains, and vegetables to maintain regular bowel function.

Pritikin Diet

Although most active cyclists tend to eat a high carbohydrate diet, this concept is pushed to the limit by the Pritikin diet.[38] This diet, or rather eating program, stresses a high intake of complex carbohydrates (75—80% of total Calories) and a marked reduction in fat and protein (each contributing 10%).

In his writings, Pritikin relates numerous testimonials from triathletes and other endurance athletes to support his claims of improved athletic performance. His concept, which amounts to continuous carbohydrate loading, is well presented and appears to be supported in practice. Aside from the somewhat monotonous nature of the meal plans, this regimen may be a reasonable consideration, both for the athlete in training and for those who feel a need to modify the high-fat Western diet. Whether or not it actually improves performance is as yet unresolved.

3
Nutrition for the Competitive Cyclist

Dedication and training remain the most effective methods of developing natural abilities. Though nutritional conditioning will never be a substitute for a demanding physical training program, it is essential to achieve and maintain top physical performance. Given two equally talented and trained competitors, a sound nutritional program can give the one that additional edge that makes a winner.

This chapter will tie together our current understanding of physiology and nutrition to present a state-of-the-art philosophy for the competitive cyclist, based on the insights gained from the material coverd in the two preceding, more theoretical chapters.

Training Diet

There is no magic dietary program for the training period. During this time, the cyclist needs a balanced diet that meets the energy requirements of the training program. The usual distribution of Calories approximates 50 % carbohydrate, 10—15% protein, and 25—35% fat. As training intensities and the total caloric replacement needs increase, the need for carbohydrate Calories will increase, while the fat and protein requirements do not change. As a result, it is not unusual for a competitive cyclist to take in 75—90% of his or her daily Calories in the form of carbohydrates.

These Calories should be eaten in a minimum of three meals a day. If caloric requirements are sufficiently high, frequent snacking may be necessary to avoid unwanted weight loss. In addition, the daily program should be structured so that a significant percentage of the Calories are taken early in the day. This anticipates and provides for the metabolic needs of the day's exercise. There is some evidence that more Calories from the evening meal are preferentially directed to fat storage, and this possibility is minimized as well. As discussed previously, the immediate post-exercise period may provide an additional opportunity for replacing muscle glycogen, and snacking during those few hours is encouraged.

Although we have seen that fat can be of importance for endurance activities, the body's normal stores are more than adequate for these needs. Only training can increase free fatty acid utilization. Increasing dietary fat has no beneficial effect to force this metabolic change. In fact, there has been suggestive evidence that a high fat diet actually decreases endurance capacity.

Proteins, although essential at a level of 40—70 grams per day, are likewise potentially harmful to a training program at higher intakes. There is no evidence that increasing protein intake above these requirements improves muscle development, and any extra protein Calories are merely metabolized into glycogen or body fat. In addition, the by-product of this metabolism, urea, requires water for its excretion by the kidneys. This not only may have a long-term negative effect on kidney function, but also exacerbates any tendency towards dehydration.

In contrast to fats and proteins, the appropriate use of carbohydrates can enhance cycling performance and is important in a training program. A high carbohydrate diet increases the amount of glycogen stored in the muscles and liver. This not only increases the duration of performance before exhaustion during the competitive event, but also has a positive effect during the training program itself.

A diet deficient in carbohydrates results in a gradual decline in muscle glycogen (stores are not completely rebuilt after each training session) and can produce a chronic state of fatigue. In addition, failure to replenish muscle glycogen has been tied in with the development of post-exercise muscle stiffness. Both can prevent an optimal progressive training regimen. To avoid these problems, it is important that the total caloric expenditures be replaced each day and that a conscious effort be made to assure that at least 600 grams, or 2400 Calories (based on potential muscle and liver glycogen stores) be in the form of carbohydrates. At this time there is no evidence that complex carbohydrates are superior to simple sugars for the glycogen repletion process.

As the total body energy stores, particularly muscle and liver glycogen, are so important to the overall success of a training program, there needs to be a close and conscious monitoring of the balance between energy expenditure and daily caloric intake. Daily weighing provides a check on this process and the body weight should be monitored each morning before an exercise that may cause a change in the state of hydration. Any progressive weight loss should lead to a reevaluation of the overall Calorie replacement program.

In preparation for the event, glycogen loading can be considered. At the extreme, this is a program of six days duration which begins with depletion of muscle glycogen by prolonged exertion, i.e. 2 to 4 hours of cycling. For the next three days, a low carbohydrate diet (100 grams of carbohydrate per day) is ingested. The last three days require a high carbohydrate diet, consisting of 60—70% carbohydrates, with at least 600 grams of carbohydrate per day. This replenishes the muscle glycogen stores and allows the supercompensation, or loading, to occur. Some athletes feel that the weight gain and muscle stiffness that occur with this program interferes with their performance and prefer to omit the initial exercise/depletion phase. In that case, the high carbohydrate diet is similar to the regimen recommended for the entire training period as described above.

A balanced diet will meet all vitamin and mineral requirements during the training period. If there is any concern about becoming deficient because of unusual dietary habits or a weight loss program, a daily multivitamin is generally considered safe. Salt replacement is usually unnecessary unless there will be and estimated fluid loss in excess of 4% BW (body weight).

Pre-Event Diet

If the cyclist has been on a good dietary regimen during the training period — daily replacement of Calories expended with an emphasis on carbohydrates, good hydration, minimal exercise for the two days before — there are no special requirements in the immediate pre-event period (the 4 hours before competition). The pre-event meal should be eaten at least 3 to 4 hours before the competition begins. Like other meals of a good training diet, this meal should be high in carbohydrate (60—70% of Calories), low in fat, and should be taken with adequate fluids. A low residue (fiber) content and a low salt content are also recommended. If liquid food is preferred, it can be taken as close as two hours prior to the event because of the more rapid stomach emptying, digestion, and absorption. This approach is preferred by some cyclists who feel it decreases nausea.

There is evidence that a carbohydrate snack immediately prior to competition (5 to 10 minutes before) is helpful in prolonging the duration of exercise to exhaustion. This is only important in events lasting more than 2 hours and presumably works by protecting muscle glycogen stores in the same manner as supplements taken while exercising. It is important to time the consumption of this snack closely, as too long an interval before the event can allow digestion, absorption, and an insulin response with resulting hypoglycemia just as the event is beginning. It is for the same reason that no meal should be eaten in the critical period 4 hours before the event.

Nutrition During the Event

Carbohydrate supplements are important during a cycling event that lasts two hours or more, but probably have no effect on performance in shorter events. There is no consensus as to the best carbohydrate formula, but it appears that liquids with up to a 10% glucose concentration are preferable. Drinks containing complex carbohydrates may give an additional edge by supplying even more carbohydrate Calories. The supplementation of fluids should be started on a preventive basis within 15 to 20 minutes of the start of the event, particularly if weather conditions are adverse — high temperatures and very high or low humidity.

It is important that carbohydrate supplements be started at the same time as the event. Once fatigue has occurred, oral glucose is much less effective in prolonging performance.[5] There may be an upper limit to how much carbohydrate supplementation the body can utilize. One study suggested that the maximum was 1 gram of glucose per minute, or 60 grams per hour (4 Calories per minute or 240 Calories per hour).[35]

Another approach to enhancing the use of both glucose stores and oral supplements is to modify the exercise intensity or the $\%\dot{V}_{Omax}$ at which one is performing. The relationship between glucose and FFAs as an energy source for exercise is not a linear one. That is, a 20% increase in $\dot{V}_{O2}$ from 50 to 70% of $\dot{V}_{O2max}$ uses less additional glucose than an increase from 70 to 90% (see Fig. 1.2). Thus an endurance athlete can utilize additional fat, covering more miles before all his body glycogen is depleted by simply slowing down slightly. This can be of particular importance if a sprint may be needed at the end of the event. As glycogen is essential for both aerobic exercise approaching 100% $\dot{V}_{O2max}$ and for any anaerobic activity, a cyclist who has used all his glycogen is truly 'out of gas.'

Fluid replacement is essential and should be started on a preventive basis within 15 to 20 minutes of the start of the event, particularly if weather conditions are adverse — high temperatures and very high or very low humidity. A fluid deficit of up to 2% BW does not appear to have an adverse effect on performance. However, at a deficit of 3% BW there is a decrease in endurance and at 4—7% BW a definitive deterioration in muscle strength. Above 6% BW life-threatening complications, such as heat exhaustion and heat stroke, can occur.

As one study demonstrated a persistent deficit in isometric and isotonic performance four hours after rehydration took place, it is probably better to anticipate and replace fluid losses on a regular basis.[21] During severe conditions of temperature or humidity, or with prolonged training and competitive sessions, regular pre- and post-event weighing can help to assess the adequacy of fluid replacement. For periods of less than four hours, any weight loss will be primarily fluid related. The stomach does have its limits, however, and it appears that 800 ml, or approximately 1 quart, is the most that can be handled per hour. This volume diminishes as exercise intensity increases; nausea and distention can occur if larger volumes are pushed.[35]

Post-Event Nutrition

If the cyclist is performing in multiple events, post-event nutritional and fluid replacement must be addressed on an individual basis, depending on the time between events. Of particular importance is the insulin effect, which may occur if less than two hours elapse between events. Once the competition has been completed, nutritional management is the same as during the training period.

Nutrition for Ultra-Endurance Events

Ultra-endurance events are becoming increasingly popular and place further demands on the human machine. Minimal nutritional modifications are needed when compared to the requirements of any cycling event over 4 hours in duration. There should be a continued emphasis on carbohydrate supplementation during the exercise period to protect endogenous stores, and the full carbohydrate loading program is of additional help in maximizing muscle glycogen prior to the event.

Enormous amounts of fluid can be lost, and fluid replacement needs scrupulous attention. One major difference is the slower pace of the event. This allows an increased use of free fatty acids by the muscle and extends muscle glycogen even further. Although training increases the efficiency of FFA use, there is no evidence that diet, either before or during the event, has any effect on this aspect of metabolism.

Recommended Nutrition Plan

Training period
1. Determine daily caloric replacement needs (Table 1.2)
2. Calculate body weight in kg (BW = 0.455 x weight in lbs)
3. Daily diet program as follows:

Protein:
1.5 x BW = grams of protein per day
Total protein Cal = g/day x 4 Cal/g

Fats:
70 g (30% of Cal in basal diet of 2000 Cal/day
600 Cal /day

Carbohydrates (CHO):
Balance of the replacement needs
(Replacement Cal — Protein Cal — Fat Cal) / (4Cal/g)
It is advantageous to replace Calories 1 to 2 hours after exercise

Pre-Competition Program

4 days prior to the event:
9 g CHO/kg BW/day (approx 600 g/day)

Balance of Cal from fat and protein (no set ratio)
Limit exercise to minimum to maintain flexibility

4 hours before:
minimum 200 g CHO meal
low fat

4 minutes before:
45 g CHO candy bar

During Competition
Regular CHO replacement (start immediately)
60 g CHO/h minimum
liquid preferred
     10% concentration optimal (equiv. to cola drink)
     complex CHO drinks permit additional Calories

Liquids:
800 ml/h

15-minute intervals (200 ml) minimum
(standard water bottle = 590 ml)

Post -Competition
600 g CHO/day x 2 days to replete glycogen
1 to 2 hours after exercise favors muscle glycogen repletion.

4
Carrying Your Calories

Now that you've made a decision on your fuel for the day, it's time to review the alternatives available for carrying it on your bike trip. There are several options — each with its own advantages and disadvantages, as summarized in Table 4.1. Although there are minor disadvantages associated with carrying food on the bike, a little planning can eliminate these rough edges. Each alternative will be evaluated for rider comfort, carrying capacity, accessibility while riding, frontal surface area, which influences the wind resistance, and the effect on overall bike handling.

Packaging and Packing

Individual packaging of each item, both solid and liquid, needs consideration first. With commercial products this is rarely a problem, since durable packaging appears to be part of successful food marketing. However, repacking foods purchased in bulk or packaging those personally prepared at home can be a challenge.

In competitive events, where even a small distraction can cost valuable seconds, packaging is a major consideration in planning for

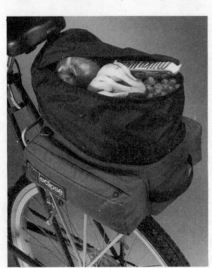

caloric replacement. For the recreational rider who intends to eat while on the bike, safety is an issue, since even a momentary lapse in concentration can lead to a fall. Finally, for those planning a relaxed outing with a stop to eat, packaging is important to prevent leaks during transportation and to maintain an appetizing appearance of the food.

There is no universal answer to the packaging challenge, as each food and type of event has its own unique requirements. In competitive events, where time is of the essence, less is truly more, and foods such as cookies and dried fruits that need no wrappers are favored. If the event allows a few additional seconds for eating, but still requires eating on the bike, loosely wrapped non-liquid items can be added to the menu. But beware of those prepackaged items that come in indestructible plastic and require two hands and scissors to open. For the picnic crowd, self-sealing Tupperware type containers are best. They come in various sizes and shapes, fitting almost any food item and at least the originals work well for liquids and semi-solids.

Once individual items have been packaged, they need to be packed for the event. For the single rider with a one-course meal this is rarely a problem, but for larger groups and multi-course meals some planning is necessary. The effect of vibration and shifting or migration of containers needs to be anticipated. This can be controlled by using picnic accessories such as napkins or a tablecloth for packing material, or with other alternatives such as loosely 'balled' newspaper and foam rubber. The latter can be precut to protect not only food containers, but also glassware for those planning the truly elegant outing.

Packaging Snacks

Packaging of small food items is an often neglected but very important part of a successful cycling nutrition program. Such aspects as transportability, accessibility, and portion size need to be considered. The snacks to be consumed while riding should be in a form that is durable and will transport well until eaten. Prepare or purchase them in bite sized pieces, and package them for easy access when needed.

Plastic sandwich bags make a simple packaging for snack foods that are durable but might crumble or melt in your pocket. They do not work well for multiple servings, as it is difficult to open the bag and separate the contents while continuing to concentrate on the road. For this reason, single portion packaging is recommended for competitive riding or whenever fast feeding on the bike is planned.

Carrying Solid Food

The jersey pocket is the simplest method of transporting food and remains the preference of competitive riders. It has the advantage of easy accessibility with minimal effects on bike handling and aerodynamics. The disadvantage lies in its limited carrying capacity. The alternative in competitive events is the musette, or food bag, handed to the riders at predetermined locations. This is suited to long distance events where the bulk and weight of the food needed to replace the Calories expended would not fit in the pockets of a cycling jersey, or might have a negative impact on performance if it were. Of all means of carrying food, the jersey pocket is the only one that allows safe and ready access to food while riding. The belt bag, or fanny pack, and the handlebar bag are alternatives for those eating on the bike, but both are less desirable from the standpoint of safety.

The fanny pack is gaining increased acceptance by competitive long distance and recreational bikers. It has been used by cross-country skiers for years and, since it is attached by a waist belt, has the advantage of leaving the shoulders and upper body free. The weight is carried quite low and thus has no effect on shoulder fatigue. This pack carries more than the pockets in the jersey, yet it can be

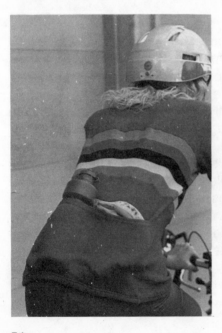

accessed while riding if needed. Although the pack is usually worn in back to eliminate any interference when assuming the aerodynamic drop position while biking, it can be pulled around to the front with minimal effort while sitting in the upright position. Then either one or both hands can be used to open the zipper and remove the food. A disadvantage is that the pack is at the same level as the jersey pockets, which essentially eliminates their use for food storage. The cumbersome maneuver described above needs to be repeated each time food is removed, and in the long run it is less efficient than using a bike pack and transferring to the jersey pockets during occasional brief stops.

The handlebar bag has the advantage of being readily accessible, and, with some caution, it can be opened while moving. It does increase wind drag and affects steering responsiveness when loaded.

There are various other packs available for carrying food on the bike, but all suffer from the disadvantage of being inaccessible while riding. The traditional backpack is one possibility, but it becomes uncomfortable on longer rides. The shoulders are a weak area for many riders, and the stress of a loaded backpack can accentuate this. As a result, it is recommended only for short trips when no alternatives are available.

Bike packs are another alternative. These can carry larger quantities and, being attached to the bike, they don't hinder the rider in any riding positions or increase body fatigue. Their disadvantages include an increase in the frontal surface area and wind drag, and a decrease in the responsiveness and maneuverability of the bike. These packs, in order of increasing capacity are the seat bag, rack-top pack, front panniers and rear panniers.

The seat bag, or saddle bag, though not as popular in the US as it is in Britain, is available in a wide variety of sizes. It can be quite small (holding no more than a spare inner tube and a candy bar) or large enough for a full meal. Being under the seat, it is relatively aerodynamic and has a minimal effect on bike handling and performance.

The rack-top pack requires a bike rack (as do panniers) and is another step up as far as equipment needs. It carries more than a handlebar bag and most seat bags, is slightly more aerodynamic in its location behind the rider and seat post, and has less effect on handling characteristics. It is my favorite to carry food for group outings.

Finally there are panniers, which have as their advantage the quantity of food and other items that can be carried. They have a significant wind drag effect, and when loaded are heavy enough to influence bike handling significantly. They are available in small versions intended to be used on the front, and as larger models intended to be used with a bike rack in the rear, though the smaller version also fits in the back.

The ultimate pack, mentioned for completeness, is the sagwagon — a car or van following the cyclists. This method of transportation allows almost unlimited carrying capacity, including the bike and rider if all is not going well. It represents the ultimate in rider comfort, as no additional weight needs to be carried on the bike or by the rider, presents no access problems, provides the ability to obtain food while moving (in the form of a quick handoff), and can actually cut down on wind drag if drafting maneuvers are considered. Its major disadvantage is a philosophical one for those cyclists who wish to be truly self-propelled. For off-road cycling, the sagwagon is of course only of very limited use, as it cannot follow the riders or meet up with them except in those places where they get back to civilization.

Table 4.1 Comparison of Carrying Gear

Item	carrying capacity	rider comfort	access	air drag	bike handling
Jersey pocket	+	−	++++	ME	ME
Backpack	+++	− − −	0	ME	−
Fanny pack	++	−	++	ME	ME
Seat pack	+	ME	0	−	ME
Handlebar bag	++	ME	+	− − −	− −
Rack pack	+++	ME	0	− −	−
Panniers	++++	ME	0	− − −	− − −

Legend to Table 4.1

ME= minimal effect
0 = no effect
+ = relatively better
− = relatively worse

Carrying Fluids

Unlike solid foods, there are limited options for carrying fluids. All re-quire a closed plastic bottle which is generally carried on the bike in a cage or rack. The cage is usually attached to either the down tube or the seat tube, but can also be attached to the handlebar stem for easier access. On occasion, the water bottle can be carried in a jer-sey pocket, usually when an additional or reserve bottle is to be used, and in this situation it should be carried in the middle pocket of the traditional three-pocket jersey to minimize the tendency to slide around to either side.

The traditional water bottle spigot is a nipple with a slide closure draining directly from the top of the bottle. This requires the bottle and head be tipped while drinking — with the attendant risk of get-ting a mouthfull of air and water when the bottle is less than full and is not tipped quite far enough. The greater danger lies in the need to take the eyes off the road while drinking this way. A major advance is the use of a drain tube extending to the bottom of the bottle, eliminating the need to tip the bottle in order to drink. It also eliminates the air surge until the bottle is empty. An additional refinement is the use of a hand bulb pump and extension tubing that allows the bottle to remain in the cage while manual air pressurization delivers fluid directly into the mouth.

5
Where to Eat

Now that we've covered the subject of what to eat for cycling and how to carry it with you, it's time to consider the topic of where to eat. As eating is essential to survival, man's development over the centuries has included the ability to eat in all positions and under almost all conditions. Since the purpose of this book is to increase the enjoyment of bicycling, and not teach basic survival techniques, a review of the this topic might prove worthwhile and provide new insights to liven up your tour.

Eating on the Bike

The most common place to eat while cycling is — you guessed it — on the bike. This goes for the recreational cyclist as well as the competitive rider. The major consideration is that of safety and the following should be kept in mind to avoid unnecessary risks:

1. Slow down.
2. Increase concentration on the road, anticipating upcoming obstacles or hazards.
3. In a pace line, eat when at the end, not in the middle or while pulling.
4. In hilly terrain, eat after you crest the hill, not while climbing.

If these simple measures are taken into consideration, it will not be necessary to stop to eat.

Roadside Shops

Bakeries are the second most common eating spots. Seasoned tourers will often use a bakery as an intermediate goal to break up the tedium of a long ride. It is wise to space these bakery stops at two hour intervals, when muscle glycogen stores are usually approaching exhaustion and need replenishing. A good tour or ride leader will often scout out the best bakeries and plan the day accordingly. These stops minimize the need to carry extra weight and bulk on the bike. In fact, it is the availability of bakeries and the associated opportunity to 'carbo replete' *en route* that provide the major incentives for many Saturday riders.

The use of bed and breakfast, or B&B, accommodations is an extension of the bakery concept for the multiple day tour. These stops provide comfortable lodgings and a pleasant breakfast before heading off for the first bakery. They minimize the need to carry camping gear and, by themselves, can provide a goal for the tour if they are in a unique setting. As with bakeries, the wise tour leader will often plan the trip around the most desirable B&Bs, knowing that the psychological diversion of the evening will often make the next day's riding that much more pleasant.

Sagwagon

When a sagwagon is being used, and particularly when the driver is someone who wants to participate in the group camaraderie but either can't or does not want to ride a bike, a modification of the B&B approach is often very successful. In this situation, the cyclists set off after deciding on a predetermined meeting point for the midday meal break. The sagwagon driver then has the option of sleeping in, lounging around, or reconnoitering the local gift shops, before setting out in the morning.

The sagwagon carries the food and whatever else is needed to provide the opportunity for a major midday meal — from a simple picnic to a regal affair with all the trimmings, including real plates, flatware, and glasses. After a relaxed lunch, the driver proceeds on to the night's lodging and again has extra time to relax before the bike group arrives. This approach opens up many new options for cycling families, particularly when there are divergent goals and abilities. The fact that a motor vehicle is available also extends the possibilities for the evening meal.

Picnic Spots

The ultimate challenge is often picking an appropriate spot for your picnic, whether supported by a sagwagon or carrying the food entirely on the bike. Fortunately, there are limitless possibilities. While bakeries are in predetermined locations, a picnic can be set almost anywhere. A quiet spot off the highway is preferable, and additional rustic trappings such as a stream or a lake can add to the atmosphere.

Most people have their own mental image of the ideal setting for a picnic, and with the miles of country roads and off-road terrain now accessible by mountain bike, you will find many superb spots along your way or just a little off the beaten track. It is this multitude of possibilities that makes bike touring and the picnics that go along with it so appealing to the adventuresome.

6
Practical Nutrition

In the first three chapters, the basic physiology required to develop a sound nutritional program for bicyclists was reviewed. Then we summarized specific packaging and transportation concerns. In this chapter we will bring together these ideas to develop a practical nutritional program for the cyclist.

Snacks and Light Meals

The foods in this category form the backbone of any serious cycling program, providing variety and an occasional psychological lift for those out on a pleasure ride. The difference between a snack and a light meal is often difficult to define, but hinges on the two factors of quantity and quality:

1. How much is eaten at any one time?
2. Do you eat on the bike or stop to do so?

The philosophy toward food breaks varies with one's goals. The recreational rider with the luxury of time will stop to enjoy, while those in the competitive mode will begin a program of snacking while on the bike early in the ride in anticipation of the delay in stomach emptying that occurs with strenuous exercise. Any Calories absorbed will delay glycogen depletion with the subsequent onset of fatigue, or the 'bonk' — the cycling equivalent of the runner's 'wall'.

The secret for maximum performance in events that last more than 2 hours (the time at which muscle glycogen depletion occurs) is to snack frequently, at least every 20—30 minutes. A successful program requires a compromise between eating enough to prevent hunger and avoiding the pitfall that 'if a little is good, a lot must be better.' The risk of the latter is stomach distention, bloating and nausea, resulting in a definite deterioration in performance.

To apply this concept to your program, refer to Table 1.3 in Chapter 1 and, based on your own goals and abilities, make a rough estimate of your caloric requirements per hour. Next, decide on an eating schedule — every 15 or 20 minutes is a practical compromise.

Then, using the food suggestions below, a specific program can be tailored to meet your caloric needs. The final step is an on-the-road test. This is essential, since physiologic and digestive functions vary from person to person and may require individual refinements to meet your specific needs or preferences.

Foods in this section can also be used in the pre-race meal. If used for that purpose, they should be eaten at least 3 hours prior to the start of the event. This assures that your stomach will be empty and that the bulk of digestion and absorption will have occurred before the stress of vigorous activity causes the inevitable slow-down in these processes.

Carrying Snacks

Packaging of these foods is an often neglected but very important part of a successful cycling nutritional program. Such things as transportability, accessibility, and portion size need to be considered. This is particularly important when the plan involves a competitive event and eating while on the bike. In that case, the food needs to be in a form that is durable and will transport well until eaten. It should be prepared in bite sized pieces, and needs to be packaged so that it is easily accessible when needed. The ideal model is the trusty banana which must have been developed by a cyclist. It transports well in a jersey pocket, resisting the destructive forces often applied to items carried there, is packaged in a biodegradable wrapper, is readily accessible using one hand and the teeth, and adapts easily to single bite portions.

As pointed out in Chapter 4, plastic sandwich bags make a simple packaging for snack foods that are durable but might crumble or melt in your pocket. They do not work well for multiple servings, as it is difficult to open the bag and separate the contents while continuing to concentrate on the road. For this reason, single portion packaging is recommended for competitive riding or wherever paceline nutrition is planned. Snacks that are readily adapted to this program include hard cookies, fig bars, apple slices, orange slices, and some hard bars such as granola bars.

Eating while on the bike takes some practice and concentration. During practice rides, the effects of a mouthfull of food on breathing, and the ease with which food can be aspirated into the windpipe, should be noted. These risks increase with exertion and for that reason eating is best avoided during strenuous climbs or pulls. If riding in a paceline, the best time to eat is after moving to the end of the line, not while in the middle of the pack, where increased concentration is needed.

Snack Survey

In the belief that there are common foods preferred by most riders, both competitive and recreational, a survey of snack foods was undertaken , including a review of several bicycling magazines, to establish what these might be. The diversity of responses was a surprise — it appears that everyone has his or her own favorite. However, there was a pattern in the groups of food. Dried fruits were the most common — presumably because of their high caloric content, the ease with which bite-sized portions could be prepared, and their relatively indestructible nature when carried on a long ride. Table 6.1 summarizes the results of this survey and include the Calories per average serving. For some perspective on this Calorie count, remember that at 15 miles per hour a 165 pound rider needs 400 Calories per hour to replace those expended.

Two prepared 'delicacies' were thought to hold promise, but the exact caloric content could not be determined due to individual variation in preparation. The first was a sandwich of jelly and cream cheese. The second, a mixture of peaches, honey, and water in a plastic bag, emphasizes that there is plenty of room for experimentation in the snack area!

There are some foods to avoid (or at least leave to the end of your experimental list). The stress of vigorous exercise has a stimulating effect on the digestive tract, and the more vigorous the exercise (or more out of shape the rider) the greater this effect. Certain foods accentuating this normal physiologic reflex include dairy products and spicy, greasy, or oily foods. Moderation is the key to success in snack planning. The best advice is to start off with small amounts of those foods that sound appealing, with your own individual response dictating the next step. Additional suggestions for snack foods can be found in Chapter 7.

Table 6.1 Preferred Bicycle Snacks

Food	Amount	Calories
cookies (generic)	2 small or 1 large	105
Fig Newton	1	50
Chips Ahoy	1	47
Oreo	1	47
Graham cracker	1	30
Animal cracker	1	8
Ginger snap	1	16
Vanilla wafer	1	19
Fresh fruit		
banana	4 oz (1 avg. size)	100
pear	4 oz	98
grapes	$1/2$ cup	57
orange	4 oz (1 avg. size)	60
apple	4 oz (1 avg. size)	80
peach	4 oz (1 avg. size)	46
cantaloupe	4 oz	36
Dried fruit		
raisins	$1/4$ cup	110
apricots	$1/4$ cup	78
prunes	$1/4$ cup	96
apples	$1/4$ cup	52
figs	$1/4$ cup	127
fruit roll-up	$1/2$ oz (1 avg. size)	50
Candy bar (generic)	1 oz	130
Gum drop	1	4
Baked potato	4 oz	110
Pastries		
doughnut	1 avg. size	125
eclair	1 avg. size	315
muffin	1 avg. size	100
toast	1 slice	60
plain bagel	1	180
Rice pudding	$1/2$ cup	160
Rice (cooked)	4 oz	130
Yoghurt	1 cup	115

Beverages

It is safe to say that the single biggest mistake of many competitive athletes is failure to replace the fluid losses associated with exercise. This is aggravated in bicycling as moving air promotes both rapid skin evaporation and a decreased sense of perspiring which, in turn, leads to a false impression of minimal fluid loss. For a successful ride, it is essential that fluid replacement be started early and continued on a regular basis.

During vigorous exercise, the sensation of thirst lags well behind your fluid replacement needs. As a result, once you notice that you are thirsty, there will already be a significant fluid deficit to overcome. On a hot day, a minimum of 4—5 ounces of fluid should be taken every 15 minutes from the start of exercise. A practical way to determine if you are taking adequate fluid replacement is to weigh yourself before and after a long ride. A drop of a pound or two won't impair performance, but greater weight loss indicates the need to change your replacement routine. As you customize a program for your personal needs, remember that a pint of liquid weighs roughly one pound.

Several factors influence your fluid needs. An obvious one is the day's temperature. If fresh fruits with a high liquid content, such as oranges, apples, grapes, or peaches, are being eaten, fluid intake can be scaled back accordingly. Alcoholic beverages should be strictly avoided. Alcohol is not only a mild diuretic, accentuating the tendency to dehydrate, but also interferes with performance through its negative effect on glucose metabolism in the liver.

Any sugar in the replacement fluids is usually considered a bonus for the cyclist. Because liquids are readily emptied from the stomach, this sugar is quickly absorbed into the blood stream and transported to the muscles, where it is available as an alternative to muscle glycogen stores. Following the same reasoning, drinks containing glucose polymers should be even more advantageous, since they permit a higher caloric 'density'— the number of Calories per oz of fluid.

There have been no studies confirming the benefits of fruit drinks (which contain the sugar fructose) over glucose drinks. Although fructose sugars are utilized by the cell with a lesser insulin response, this appears to be of minimal, if any, practical value. Thus, taste alone appears to be the advantage of fruit drinks.

Until recently, it was thought that a 2.5% concentration of glucose or glucose polymer molecules was the maximum tolerated by the digestive tract before delays in stomach emptying and subsequent nausea occurred. However, a 40% solution of honey and tea has been the standard for years in competitive cross-country skiing. A recent study on cyclists has shown normal stomach emptying with 6—8% solutions, but when the concentrations were pushed above 11%, the expected nausea occurred.[51]

In summary, drinking plain water at a rate of 1 quart per hour is adequate for rides of $1^1/2$ to 2 hours. On longer rides, where the body's glycogen stores will be approaching exhaustion, glucose supplements assume increased importance. An 8 to 10 % sugar concentration appears to be the maximum tolerated before delays in stomach emptying occur. Glucose polymers offer the advantage that the number of Calories per quart can be increased without an unpalatable sweet taste. Table 6.2 compares the commercial drinks currently available. It is interesting to note that the old standbys, such as apple juice and cola drinks, have that magic maximum concentration of 10% and are very cost effective per Calorie provided.

The physiological benefits, if any, of glucose polymers over simple sugars in replacement drinks, are still being clarified. Although there is little question that more Calories can be ingested per quart of fluid, there has not been a clear performance advantage when evaluated under controlled conditions.[51] At this time, the major benefit of these polymers appears to be the absence of the sweet taste and nauseating properties of high-concentration glucose drinks, eliminating this barrier to maintaining a high fluid intake.

Picnic and Gourmet Food

Foods in this category — recipes for which are also given in Chapter 7 — will mainly be of interest to recreational cyclists, particularly those who 'bike to eat'. This group appreciates the rewards that go with maintaining fitness and replacing the Calories burned with aerobic exercise. Some of these foods can also be adapted for endurance activity, particularly if taste fatigue develops from 'the same old foods' on those long century rides. Be warned, however, that the higher fat content in some recipes makes them not only heavy to carry on the bike for a long trip, but may also create the same sensation in the stomach.

The picnic ride is a gala social occasion compared to training sessions and competitive cycling. This is the event that appeals to the

Table 6.2 Comparison of sports drinks (courtesy BICYCLING) [51]

Sports Drink	Main Ingredients	Recommended Concentration	Sodium*	Other Electrolytes*	Calories*	Cost ($)*
BODY FUEL 100	Glucose Polymers	0.3%	63 mg	None	13	.81
BODY FUEL 450	Glucose Polymers / Fructose	4%	200 mg	Potassium - 50 mg	100	.57
CARBO PLUS	Glucose Polymers	16%	13 mg	Potassium - 250 mg / Magnesium - 250 mg	425	1.83
EXCEED — FLUID REPLACEMENT AND ENERGY DRINK	Glucose Polymers (Polycose brand) / Fructose	7.2%	165 mg	Potassium - 140 mg / Magnesium - 15 mg	170	.73
FILA FITNESS	Fructose / Sucrose	6.9%	138 mg	Potassium - 38 mg / Chloride - 244 mg	139	1.25
GATORADE	Sucrose / Glucose	6%	275 mg	Potassium - 63 mg	125	.99
GOOKINAID E.R.G.	Glucose	5.7%	175 mg	Potassium - 250 mg	113	.47
MAX	Glucose Polymers	7.5%	38 mg	None	175	.47
PRIPPS PLUSS	Sucrose	7.4%	163 mg	Potassium - N/A	175	.47
RECHARGE	Fructose (From fruit juices)	7.6%	75 mg	Potassium - 213 mg	180	.99
RPM ENERGY DRINK	Fructose	7.6%	0 mg	Potassium - 175 mg	175	.62
TOUR DE FRANCE CARBOPLEX II	Glucose Polymers / Fructose	5.9%	6 mg	None	113	.45
TOUR DE FRANCE REHYDRATE	Fructose	4.4%	250 mg	Potassium - 175 mg	100	.47
ULTRA-ENERGY	Glucose Polymers / Sucrose / Lactose / Dextrose	23%	N/A	Magnesium - N/A / Calcium - N/A / Potassium - N/A	500	5.00
VITALADE	Fructose	10%	0 mg	Potassium - 233 mg	215	.78
CARBONATED COLA	High-fructose corn syrup; Sucrose	10.4%	25 mg	Potassium - 6.2 mg / Magnesium - 6.2 mg	260	.83
APPLE JUICE	Fructose / Glucose	11.7%	20 mg	Potassium - 740 mg / Magnesium - 20 mg	300	.95

*Per standard 20-oz. water bottle filled to top.

whole family and those friends who only occasionally ride a bike. To the non-cyclist, the picnic becomes the main focus, while the bicycling itself remains an excuse for the outing. An additional benefit of the modest exercise associated with the ride, as opposed to vigorous exercise, is that it stimulates the appetite and enhances the taste of the meal that follows.

Packaging is often a major problem for the picnic cyclist. It is often easier to bring the raw materials and create the finished product on site, rather than attempt to transport the completed dish. The best results are obtained if one keeps an open and innovative mind, uses containers that approximate the size and the shape of the food being prepared, and sticks with self-sealing containers such as Tupperware. If all else fails, remember that every meal on a picnic or camping trip tastes like gourmet fare, even if it's a little lopsided.

Bacterial growth and food poisoning can be a problem with some foods if they are not prepared and handled properly. This applies especially to dairy products, poultry, eggs, fish, mayonnaise, and cream-filled pastries. The associated risk is minimized by following several simple steps. First, by preparing the food properly, using clean utensils and fresh ingredients, the chances of bacterial contamination are reduced. The second line of defense is complete cooking, which kills any bacteria that may be present. Finally, keeping the food cool after preparation slows down the growth of any bacteria that have escaped the initial two steps. It is essential to keep your prepared foods refrigerated until the last possible minute and use insulated styrofoam containers for transportation to help keep them cool. Even with these precautions, it is best to eat prepared foods within four to six hours of preparation or refrigeration.

Picnic Types

There are three different philosophies for the bicycling picnic — the spontaneous picnic, the brown bag picnic, and the elegant picnic. The spontaneous or minimalist approach emphasizes off-the-shelf foods, and such a meal can be put together in any supermarket or grocery store. It includes ready-to-eat items such as cheese, nuts, crackers, bread, canned paté, marinated mushrooms or artichokes, fruits, vegetables, and dips.

The brown bag picnic is centered around a sandwich of fresh bread and sliced meats assembled at the picnic site. For an extra touch, a salad can be easily prepared, with a dressing added later to help keep it fresh. While this picnic can also be planned while walking the aisles of the supermarket, it is of immeasurable help to have access to a good delicatessen.

Finally, there is the elegant, or gourmet, picnic. This is the epitome of cycling picnics and requires prior planning and preparation time in the kitchen. Of course, any ingredients mentioned above for the spontaneous picnic can be included in this meal as well.

To aid in preparing the menu, whether minimalist or gourmet, the picnic is divided into four courses. These include:

1. appetizer or soup
2. main course
3. dessert
4. beverage

If you have an item in mind for each course, you're on your way to a successful outing.

After the menu has been completed, the food prepared or purchased, and the group is ready to set off for the memorable event,

the final checklist should be consulted. This is essential for successful picnic planning and has saved many an outing (and friendship).
The following covers the necessities:

1. ground sheet or tablecloth
2. utensils, plates, and glasses/cups
3. bottle opener (or corkscrew)
4. thermos (or ice) for cold drinks
5. sharp knife
6. light cutting board or serving platter
7. napkins, paper towels (washcloth in ziploc bag)
8. candles, matches
9. trash bag
10. insect repellent, suntan cream — or, where the climate
    dictates it, rain shelter

Now that you have all the ingredients together, you're on your way
to a pleasant aspect of biking that's often overlooked — the bicycle
picnic. Enjoy!

7
Recipe Section

In this final chapter, you will find a collection of recipes of various kinds that are particularly suitable for cycling snacks, drinks and picnics.

Remark

The recipes marked with asterisks (* —— *) are those that can be prepared easily away from home, while the others require more extensive preparation in the kitchen.

Snack Recipes

George's Bars

$1/4$ lb margarine or butter
4 eggs, beaten
1 cup flour (optional: $1/2$ as whole wheat flour)
$1/2$ teaspoon baking powder
1 teaspoon salt
$1^3/4$ cup sugar (optional: $1/2$ as brown sugar)
2 cups dates (or raisins, other dried fruits)
$2^1/2$ cups chopped walnuts
3 tablespoons molasses (optional)

Melt butter and cool slightly.

Add eggs.

Sift together flour, baking powder, salt and sugar and add to eggs/shortening mix.

Combine fruits/nuts with batter.

Spread approximately 1 inch thick in 2 greased pans.

Bake 30 min at 350 degrees F.

Cool, cut into bars.

Crispie Treats

$1/4$ cup margarine or butter
10 oz package (about 40) regular marshmallows
6 cups toasted rice cereal
1 cup raisins or dried fruit (optional)
1 cup peanuts or other nuts (optional)

Melt butter or margarine in large saucepan over low heat.

Add marshmallows and stir until completely melted.

Remove from heat.

Add cereal. Stir until well coated.

Using buttered spatula, press mixture into 13 x 9 x 2 inch pan.

Cut when cool.

Muffins

Muffins may come closest to the ideal cycling snack. They are high in carbohydrate and allow the flexibility to add, subtract, or substitute ingredients to meet individual tastes. In addition, they are easy to carry and are an ideal single portion size.

Oatmeal Raisin Muffins

$1^1/2$ cups flour (whole wheat if desired)
1 cup uncooked oatmeal
1 tablespoon baking powder
3 tablespoons sugar (or 2 tablespoons honey)
$^1/2$ cup raisins (or other dried fruit)
$^1/4$ cup walnuts (optional)
1 egg (or 2 egg whites)
1 cup milk
$^1/4$ cup vegetable oil (or $^1/2$ stick melted margarine)

Preheat oven to 400 degrees F.

Combine flour, oatmeal, baking powder, sugar, fruit, nuts.

In a separate bowl, beat egg, then stir in milk and oil.

Add liquid mixture to flour and stir until coarsely blended.

Pour into 12 muffin tins lined with paper.

Bake 15 to 20 minutes.

Carrot Muffins

$1^1/2$ cups flour (whole wheat if desired)
$^1/2$ cup uncooked oatmeal
$^1/2$ cup brown sugar
1 tablespoon baking powder
1 cup carrots, finely shredded
$^1/4$ cup nuts (wallnuts, sunflour seeds — optional)
2 eggs
$^1/4$ cup vegetable oil (or $^1/2$ stick melted margarine)
$^1/4$ cup milk

Preheat oven to 400 degrees F.

Combine flour, oatmeal, baking powder, and brown sugar.

Add carrots and nuts.

In a separate bowl, beat egg, then stir in milk and oil.

Add liquid mixture to flour and stir until coarsely blended.

Pour into 12 muffin tins lined with paper.

Bake 15 to 20 minutes.

Apple Muffins

2 cups flour (whole wheat if desired)
1 teaspoon cinnamon
1 tablespoon baking powder
1 egg (or 2 egg whites)
$1/4$ cup honey (or $1/2$ cup brown sugar)
$3/4$ cup milk
$1/4$ cup vegetable oil (or $1/2$ stick melted margarine)
1 cup shredded apple

Preheat oven to 400 degrees F.

Combine flour, baking powder, and cinnamon.

In a separate bowl, beat egg, then stir in milk, oil, honey, and apple.

Add liquid mixture to flour and stir until coarsely blended.

Pour into 12 muffin tins lined with paper.

Bake 15 to 20 minutes.

Apple–Caramel Rolls

For those with more of a sweet tooth, these caramel rolls should fill
the bill. However, because of the caramel frosting, they offer more of
a challenge to eat while on the bike than muffins.

$1/2$ cup + $1/4$ cup packed brown sugar
$1/2$ cup margarine + 2 tablespoons softened margarine
36 pecan halves
2 cups Buisquick baking mix
$1/2$ cup cold water
1 cup finely chopped apple

Preheat oven to 450 degrees F.

Place 2 teaspoons brown sugar, 2 teaspoons margarine, and 3 pecan halves in each of 12 muffin cups and melt in oven.

Mix baking mix and water until soft dough forms, then beat vigorously for 20 strokes.

Smooth dough into a ball on floured board.

Knead 5 times.

Roll dough into a rectangle approx. 15 x 9 inches.

Spread 2 tablespoons of margarine, $1/4$ cup brown sugar, and apple on the rectangle of dough and roll up tightly.

Cut into twelve $1^1/4$ inch wide slices.

Place slices, cut side down, in muffin cups.

Bake 10 minutes.

Invert immediately on a heatproof serving plate.

Beverage Recipes

In addition to regular fruit juices, there are many suitable ready-made commercial drinks listed in Table 6.2. Two easy-to-prepare fluid favorites are the following:

Koolaide — Add $1/4$ of the amount of sugar suggested on the package instructions and up to $1/4$ teaspoon salt per quart.

Tea — Use any regular green or black tea or, if you prefer, either a spiced tea or a herb tea. Sweeten to taste with up to $1/4$ cup sugar per quart.

Appetizer and Soup Recipes

Gazpacho

3 large ripe tomatoes
1 red pepper
1 medium yellow onion
1 large shallot
1 large cucumber
$1/4$ cup red wine vinegar
$1/4$ cup olive oil
$3/4$ cup canned tomato juice
1 egg, lightly beaten
cayenne pepper, salt, black pepper
$1/4$ cup chopped fresh dill

Wash, core, and coarsely chop vegetables.
Seed cucumber.
Mix vinegar, olive oil, canned tomato juice, and egg.
Using a blender or food processor, puree vegetables.
Add vinegar mixture.
Add cayenne, black pepper, and salt to taste.
Chill.

serves 4

Vichyssoise

3 tablespoons unsalted butter
4 large leeks, whites only, thinly sliced
1 small yellow onion, thinly sliced
4 potatoes, peeled and thinly sliced
3 cups chicken stock
$3/4$ tablespoon lemon juice
$1^1/2$ cup milk
2 cups whipping cream
pepper, salt

Melt butter and sauté leeks and onion.
Add potatoes, chicken stock, and lemon juice.
Boil for 1 hour and then cool.
Process in food processor or blender.
Return to pot , then add milk and one half of the cream.
Season to taste with pepper and salt.
Bring to a simmer for 1 minute.
Remove from heat, cool and then refrigerate.
Chill and add remaining cream just prior to serving.

serves 6

Lemon Soup

8 cups chicken broth
4 eggs
juice of 2 lemons
salt and pepper

Heat broth — simmer 20 minutes.
Beat eggs and lemon juice together until well blended.
Pour into broth slowly while stirring — do not boil.
Heat until thickened — do not boil.
Season to taste, then chill.

serves 8

Mushroom Salad with Mustard Vinaigrette

$1/4$ cup Dijon style mustard
$1/4$ cup wine vinegar
$1/2$ teaspoon dried oregano, crushed
$1/4$ teaspoon salt
$1/4$ teaspoon pepper
$1/2$ cup olive oil or salad oil
12 oz ($4^1/2$ cups)fresh mushrooms, sliced
$1/2$ cup pitted olives, halved

Combine mustard, vinegar, oregano, salt, and pepper in a large bowl.

Using a wire whisk, blend in oil.

Stir in mushrooms and olives.

Cover and chill at least 2 hours.

May be served with tomato slices and watercress sprig.

Serves 4

Carrot-Yoghurt Salad

    1 pound carrots, coarsely shredded
    2 medium apples, grated
    1 cup yoghurt
    1 tablespoon honey (optional)
    juice from one lemon
    salt, pepper
    1 tablespoon sesame seeds (optional)
    $1/4$ cup sunflower seeds, almonds, cashews (optional)
    $1/2$ cup celery, minced finely (optional)
    $1/2$ cup pineapple (optional)

Combine ingredients.

Chill.

serves 4

Cole Slaw

    4 cups cabbage, finely shredded
    2 carrots, grated
    $1/2$ cup yogurt
    $1/2$ cup mayonnaise
    3 tablespoons vinegar
    salt, pepper
    $1/2$ cup green pepper, minced (optional)
    $1/2$ cup red onion, thinly sliced (optional)

Combine ingredients.

Chill.

Let stand several hours before serving.

serves 6

* Fresh Fruit Salad *

    1 small container yogurt or sour cream
    1 apple
    1 small package raisins
    1 small package shredded coconut (optional)
    1 banana
    1 package ground nuts (optional)

Core and chop apple.

Peel and slice banana.

Mix all ingredients with sour cream or yogurt.

serves 2

* Fresh Vegie Salad *

Fresh seasonal vegetables as available, such as:

    carrots, celery, cauliflower,broccoli, radishes, tomatoes.
    1 small head of lettuce (optional)
    1 small bottle salad dressing of your choice

Chop vegetables and lettuce.

Add dressing.

Serves 1 or more, depending on quantities used

Richard's Paté

    1 large onion
    1 stick celery
    $1/2$ teaspoon garlic, crushed
    $3/4$ lb chicken livers

$^1/_2$ lb white meat of chicken
$^1/_4$ cup walnuts, toasted
$^1/_4$ cup raisins
2 teaspoons paté spice (see next recipe)
2 tablespoons Madeira
2 tablespoons cognac
$^1/_4$ lb unsalted butter

Grate onion and celery in food processor.
Sauté onion, celery, and garlic in one third of the butter.
Return to the food processor with steel blade.
Sauté chicken livers in one third of the butter and add to food processor.
Sauté white meat of chicken and add to food processor.
Add walnuts, raisins, paté spice, Madeira, cognac, and remainder of butter to the food processor.
Blend until coarsely mixed, place in paté pan, and refrigerate.

Serve with French baguettes (crusty bread) and unsalted butter.
Cornichons (small French pickles) add a nice extra touch.

Serves 8—12 as an appetizer, 4—6 as a light meal

Paté Spice (for preceding recipe)

$1^1/_2$ teaspoon bay leaves
$1^1/_2$ teaspoon f thyme
$1^1/_2$ teaspoon rosemary
$1^1/_2$ teaspoon basil
$2^1/_2$ teaspoon cinnamon
$1^1/_2$ teaspoon mace
$^3/_4$ teaspoon ground cloves
$^1/_4$ teaspoon allspice
$^1/_2$ teaspoon ground white pepper
1 teaspoon paprika

Mix herbs and finely crush them in a spice mortar.
Sift through fine sieve.
Add powdered spices.

Store in a tightly closed jar.

* Raw Vegetables *

Use any crisp vegetables that can be eaten uncooked, such as:
   carrots, celery, broccoli, cauliflower, radishes

Wash.
Remove inedible portions.
Cut into easily manageable pieces.

* Fresh Fruit *

Use fresh seasonal fruit as available, such as:
   apples, grapes, melons

Wash.
Remove rind or skins that would be difficult to manage on the bike.
Core, if appropriate, and cut into manageable pieces.

Serve with cheese if desired.

Chilled Braised Asparagus with Vinaigrette

   1 bunch asparagus (1 pound)
   pan of ice water
   vinaigrette (see next recipe)

Bring pot of salted water to a boil.
Drop in asparagus spears.
Cook until desired tenderness — don't overcook.
When tender, transfer to ice water.
Stand until cool, drain, and pat dry.
Refrigerate for 1 day maximum.
Add vinaigrette prior to serving.

Serves 4

Vinaigrette (for preceding recipe)

1 tablespoon Dijon style mustard
4 tablespoons red wine vinegar
1 teaspoon granulated sugar
^{1}/2 teaspoon salt
^{1}/2 teaspoon ground black pepper
^{1}/2 cup olive oil

Whisk mustard with vinegar, sugar, salt, and pepper.
Add olive oil while continuing to whisk.
Adjust seasonings to taste.

Makes 1 cup

Eric's Soft Pretzels

Makes a good fresh bread to eat with any of the above.

1 package yeast
1 ^{1}/2 cups warm water
1 teaspoon salt
1 tablespoon sugar
4 cups flour
1 egg, beaten
coarse salt

Measure warm water into large bowl and add yeast.
Add sugar, salt, and flour.
Mix and knead.
Place pretzels on greased cookie sheet.
Brush with egg and sprinkle with coarse salt.
Bake at 425 degrees F for 12 to 15 minutes.

Serves 4—6 (depends how far you've ridden)

Main Course Recipes

Thogh the first two recipes in this section are salads in concept, they are really light meals in their own right.

Larry's Artichoke Pasta Salad

This is only one of many pasta salad options — vary this recipe using the ingredients at hand and your imagination.

4 oz (about 1 cup) of medium sized pasta
1 jar (6 oz) marinated artichoke hearts
$^1/4$ pound small mushrooms
1 cup cherry tomatoes, halved
1 cup medium-sized ripe pitted olives
$^1/2$ teaspoon dry basil leaves
salt, pepper

Cook pasta, drain, rinse with cold water, and drain again.
Mix pasta, artichokes with their liquid, mushrooms, tomatoes, olives, and basil in a large bowl.
Toss gently.
Refrigerate for at least 4 hours.
Season with salt and pepper to taste before serving.

Serves 6

Aunt Jan's High Fiber Rice Salad

$^1/3$ cup pinenuts
$^1/3$ cup almonds
$^1/3$ cup hazelnuts
$^1/3$ cup pumpkin seeds
1 cup wild rice
1 cup brown rice
$^1/2$ cup sliced green onions
$^1/2$ cup currants
$^1/2$ cup non-fat yoghurt
wine vinegar

olive oil
cayenne pepper (very important) and salt

Toast and coarsely chop pinenuts, almonds, hazelnuts, and
pumpkin seeds.
Cook rice.
Mix nuts, rice, onions, celery, and currants.
Add wine vinegar, olive oil, cayenne pepper, and salt to the
yoghurt to make a dressing to you taste.
Add yoghurt dressing to mixture and serve with Pita bread.

Serves 2—4

Split Pea — Parmesan Spread

1 cup cooked green split peas
2 tablespoons mayonnaise
2 tablespoons Parmesan cheese
2 tablespoons low fat cottage cheese
$1/2$ teaspoon salt
1 teaspoon dry onion flakes

Mash split peas.
Mix with other ingredients.
Serve with Pita Bread.

Serves 2

Grilled Lemon Chicken

1 chicken, quartered or cut up
1 lemon, sliced
3 cloves garlic, crushed
$1/2$ cup oil, preferably olive oil
salt and pepper to taste

The day before serving, marinate in a shallow pan with lemon, oil,
salt, and pepper.
Grill over charcoal.

May be serve chilled or warm. Travels well.

Serves 4

Chicken, Cheese, and Chile Rolls à la Bruce

2 whole chicken breasts, halved
$1/2$ cup dry sherry
$2^1/2$ cups chicken broth
4 tablespoons prepared mustard
$1/2$ teaspoon garlic salt
pinch of dried sage, basil, and thyme
4 large slices jack cheese
4 strips canned peeled green chiles
4 frozen puff pastry shells
1 egg white, beaten
sesame seeds

Poach chicken breasts about 20 minutes in sherry and broth.
Cool in poaching liquid for 30 minutes.
Remove skin and bones, then refrigerate.
Mix mustard and dry seasonings.
Spread 1 tablespoon of mixture over each piece of chicken.
Wrap a slice of cheese and chile around each piece.
Let puff pastry stand at room temperature for 30 minutes.
Roll each shell into an 8-inch circle (on lightly floured board).
Place piece of wrapped chicken on shell, seam side down; bring
up sides of pastry, overlap, moisten, and pinch.
Place bundles, seam down, on ungreased cookie sheet.
Brush with egg whites and sprinkle with seeds.
Chill 30 minutes.
Bake at 425 degrees F for 30 minutes or until brown and crisp.
Cool on rack and then chill.

Makes 4

Sandwich and Quick Meal Recipes

* Sandwiches *

Here are a few examples of suitable sandwiches for eating on the bike or at the picnic site. Be guided by your own imagination and the contents of your bread bin and refrigerator (or what's available along the way).

Cream cheese on brown bread
Cream cheese and cucumbers on crustless white bread
Swiss or Dutch cheese on French bread or brown bread
Pastrami and Swiss on rye
Roast beef on white bread

* Cracker Sandwiches *

Crackers or similar crisp breads can be used instead of bread for a large variety of crunchy sandwiches. Again, just a few examples, to get you started. Butter or margarine may be helpful in bonding the various ingredients together if they are hard cheeses, such as Swiss, Dutch or American non-processed cheese. Use the bread of your choice with any of the following:

soft or hard cheese
cream cheese and jelly
processed cheese and jelly
salami and cheese

Cold Baked Potatoes

Another high-carbohydrate snack or main meal course that is easy to prepare and carry. Baked potatoes are particularly easy to make in the micro-wave oven. If you intend to eat on the bike, you may want to remove the peel beforehand.

Make with any one of various toppings, limited only by your imagination. Unless eaten on the bike, the topping is best kept separate until it's time to eat.

Dessert Recipes

Arlene's Creamy Rice Pudding

    1 cup rice
    6 cups hot milk
    1 teaspoon salt
    2 tablespoons butter
    2 teaspoons vanilla
    2 teaspoons sugar

Place all ingredients in a large pot, holding at least 8 cups.

Cook over low heat (do not boil) for 1 hour.

Remove and cool, then refrigerate.

Excellent by itself or served with seasonal fruits.

Serves 6

French Apple and Bread Pudding

    $1/4$ cup raisins or currants
    1 large tart cooking apple
    $1/4$ cup melted butter
    4 beaten eggs
    $1^3/4$ cups milk
    $1/2$ cup heavy cream
    $1/2$ cup sugar
    $1/2$ teaspoon vanilla
    2 cups unseasoned croutons or stale, dried bread
    $1/3$ cup slivered almonds
    $1/8$ cup brown sugar

Soak raisins or currants in small amount of water.

Peel, core, and thinly slice apple.

Cook apple slices in butter until translucent, then spoon into
$1^1/2$-quart casserole.

Beat eggs and then add milk, cream, sugar, and vanilla.

Add croutons (cubed dried bread), currants, and remaining butter to casserole.

Stir to mix with apples.

Pour egg mixture into casserole and let stand 20 minutes.

Sprinkle with nuts and brown sugar.

Place casserole in large pan of water in oven.

Bake at 350 degrees F for 40 minutes (or until knife comes out clean).

Serves 6

Apricot Cobbler

$1^1/2$ cups all purpose flour
scant $^1/4$ teaspoon salt
9 tablespoons unsalted butter
$^1/4$ cup shortening
$2^1/2$ cups fresh ripe apricots
1 large tart apple — peeled, cored, and sliced
1 cup sugar

In a food processor, process flour, salt, and 5 tablespoons of butter that has been frozen previously in small pieces.

Add $^1/4$ cup ice water and process until dough begins to cling together — about 10 seconds.

Drop apricots in boiling water for 10 seconds then peel, pit, and cut into $^1/2$ inch wide slices.

Roll dough into a large circle and fit into a $1^1/2$ to 2 quart baking dish.

Place apricots into dough.

Cover with sugar and dot with 4 tablespoons butter.

Place in preheated 450 degrees F oven and reduce to 425 degrees.

Bake for 45 minutes.

Serves 6 hungry bikers

* Fresh Fruit and Cheese *

Use any seasonal fruits such as:

grapes, apples, pears, plums, figs, berries, melons
any kind of non-process cheese

Wash the fruit.
Peel and core as appropriate.
Combine the fruit with the cheese.
May be prepared either at home or on site.

* Yoghurt with Toppings*

1 container of yoghurt — plain or flavor of choice
fresh seasonal fruits as available — berries are great
granola — packaged granola cereals work well here
chopped nuts
toasted coconut

Mix yoghurt with toppings of your choice — limited only by your imagination.

* Berries on Shortcake *

1 package shortcakes (known as shortbread in Britain)
fresh berries as available (e.g. strawberries, raspberries, or
blackberries)
1 can whipped cream

Shortcakes are particularly durable and the berries can then be added at the picnic site. The whipped cream really hits the spot after a few hours on the bike.

Appendix

Appendix A. Energy Requirements

Expressed in terms of the number of Calories ingested

1. Level Surface (Eh = Energy required-horizontal)

$P_w =$ $(v \times 3.509) + (.2581 \times v^2)$
$P_c =$ $P_w / 4186.8$
$C_e =$ $P_c \times T$
$C_i =$ $C_e / E = E_h$

where:

$P_w =$ power (watts)
$v =$ velocity , or speed (m/sec)
$P_c =$ power (Cal/sec)
$T =$ time
$C_e =$ Calories expended at the pedals
$C_i =$ Calories ingested = E_h
$E =$ efficiency of the human machine (approx. 25%)

Assumptions:
  75 kg rider
  10 kg bike
  level surface
  no head wind

Definitions and conversion factors:

1 watt =   1 joule/second
1 Cal =   1000 cal = 4186.8 joules = 4186.8 watts

2. Climbing Vertical Distance (E_v = Energy Required-vertical)

W =   F x D

C_e =   W/CF

C_i = $C_e/E = E_v$

where:

W =	work (ft-lbs or kgm)
F =	Force from gravity (lbs or kg)
D =	distance vertically (ft or m)
C_e =	Calories expended at the pedals
CF =	conversion factor of 3097 or 418 (for English and International units, respectively)
C_i =	Calories ingested = E_v
E =	efficiency of the human machine (approx. 25%)

Definitions and conversion factors:

1 Cal	=	1000 cal	= 184.6 joules
1 joule	=	74 ft-lb	= 0.10 kgm
1 Cal	=	3097 ft-lb	= 418 kgm

3. Total Energy Requirements in Hilly Terrain

E_t = $E_h + E_v$

where:

E_t =   Total energy requirements of cycling up a hill
(in Calories ingested)

E_h =   Energy requirements for horizontal distance covered
(in Calories ingested)

E_v =   Energy requirements for vertical distance climbed
(in Calories ingested)

Example:

A 165-pound cyclist (75 kg) rides a 10 mile hilly route at an average speed of 15 miles/hour (6.7 meters/sec). During the ride, he climbs 1500 feet (457 meters). His bicycle weighs 22 pounds (10 kg). How many Calories will he need to eat to replace the energy expended?

$$P_w = 6.7 \, [3.509 + 0.2581 \, (6.7)^2]$$
$$= 6.7 \, [3.509 + 11.586]$$
$$= 101 \text{ watts}$$

$$P_c = 101 \, / \, 4186.8 = 0.024 \text{ Cal/sec}$$

$$T = 10 \, / \, 15 = 0.66 \text{ hour}$$
$$= 0.66 \times 3600$$
$$= 2376 \text{ sec}$$

$$C_e = 0.024 \times 2376 = 57 \text{ Cal}$$

$$C_i = 57 \text{ Cal} \, / \, 0.25 = 228 \text{ Cal} = E_h$$

$$W = 85 \text{ kg} \times 457 \text{ meters}$$
$$= 38845 \text{ kgm}$$

$$C_e = 38845 \, / \, 418 = 92 \text{ Cal}$$

$$C_i = 92 \, / \, 0.25 = 371 \text{ Calories} = E_v$$

$$E_t = E_h + E_v$$
$$= 228 \text{ Cal} + 371 \text{ Cal}$$
$$= 9 \text{ Cal needed to replace those expended.}$$

If one is a purist, 50 Cal/hour need to be added for basal metabolism.

Since this ride took $^2/_3$ of an hour, the correct approximation is $599 + (^2/_3 \times 50) = 632$ Calories.

Appendix B. International Units

Scientific measurements can be expressed in several ways. English units (pound, inch) are still in common use in the United States. The rest of the world, including Britain, uses the International System of Units (SI units). The latter is based on the metric system (kilogram, centimeter) and is used in most scientific texts. In order to avoid confusion, the more common English units are used in this text, followed in parenthesis by the equivalent in SI units.

Conversion Table

1 inch	=	2.54 centimeters
1 foot	=	0.305 meters
	=	30.5 cm
1 mile	=	1.609 m
	=	1.609 km
1 mph	=	1.609 km/hr
	=	0.445 m/sec
1 ounce	=	28.35 grams
1 pound	=	454 grams (mass)
	=	4.5 N (Newton) (force)
1 quart	=	947 cubic centimeters
	=	0.947 liter
1 watt	=	1 joule/second
	=	0.014 Kilocalories/min
	=	0.014 Cal/min
1 joule	=	0.74 ft-lb
	=	1 Nm (corresponding to approximately 0.1 kgm under normal sea-level gravitational effects)
1 Calorie	=	3097 ft-lb
	=	1kcal
	=	1000 cal
	=	418 kgm
	=	4184.6 joules (J)
	=	4.18 kilojoules (kJ)

Bibliography

1. Anderson, J. and B.L. Becker. "Carbohydrate Power," *Rx Being Well* (Sept./Oct. 1987): 41—45.

2. Askew, E.W. "Role of Fat Metabolism in Exercise," *Clinics in Sports Medicine* 3 (July 1984): 605—621.

3. Burke, E., H.R. Perez, and P. Hodges. *Inside the Cyclist.* Battleboro: Velo News Corporation, 1986.

4. Casal, D.C., and A.S. Leon. "Metabolic Effects of Caffeine on Submaximal Exercise Performance in Marathoners." *Med. Sci. Sports Exer.* 14 (1982): 176

5. Coggan, A.R. and E.F. Coyle. "Reversal of Fatigue During Prolonged Exercise by Carbohydrate Infusion of Ingestion." *J. Appl. Physiol.* 63 (1987): 2388—2395.

6. Costill, D.L. "Carbohydrates for Exercise: Dietary Demands for Optimal Performance." *Int. J. Sports Med.* 9 (1988): 1—18.

7. Costill, D.L. "Water and Electrolyte Requirements During Exercise," *Clinics in Sports Medicine* 3 (July 1984): 639—648.

8. Costill, D.L., W. M. Sherman, W.J. Fink et al. "The Role of Dietary Carbohydrates in Muscle Glycogen Resynthesis after Strenuous Running." *Amer. J. Clin. Nutr.* 34 (1981): 1831—1836.

9. Coyle, E.F. "Ergogenic Aids," *Clinics in Sports Medicine* 3 (July 1984): 731–742.

10. Coyle, E.F. personal communication.

11. Coyle, E.F., A.R. Coggan, M.K. Hemmert et al. "Muscle Glycogen Utilization During Prolonged Strenuous Exercise When Fed Carbohydrate." *J. Appl. Physiol.* 61 (1986): 165—172.

12. Coyle, E.F., A.R. Coggan, M.K. Hemmert, R.C. Lowe, and T.J. Walters. "Substrate Usage During Prolonged Exercise Following a Pre-exercise Meal." *J. Appl. Physiol.* 59 (1985): 429—433.

13. Dohm, G.L. "Protein Nutrition for the Athlete," Clinics in Sports Medicine 3 (July 1984): 595—604.

14. Dohm, G.L., R.T. Beeker, R.G. Israel, and E.B. Tapscott. "Metabolic Responses to Exercise after Fasting." *J. Appl. Physiol.* 61 (1986): 1363—1368.

15. Elliot, D.L., and L. Goldberg. "Nutrition and Exercise." *Med. Clin. N. Amer.* 69 (1985): 71—82.

16. "Exercise Slows GI Transit." *Gastroenterology Observer* 6 (1987): 7.

17. Faria, I.E. "Applied Physiology of Cycling." *Sports Medicine* 1 (1984): 187–204.

18. Gollnick, P.D., and H. Matoba. "Role of Carbohydrate in Exercise,"

Clinics in Sports Medicine 3 (July 1984): 583—593.

19. Dr. Gwinup, Divn. of Endocrinology and Metabolism, UC Irvine Med. Ctr., as presented at 37th. Annual Obeisity and Assoc. Cond. Symposium.

20. Hargreaves, M., D.L. Costill, A. Coggan, I. Nishibata, and W.J. Fink. "Carbohydrate Feedings and Exercise Performance." *Med. Sci. Sports Exer.* 15 (1983): 129.

21. Hecker, A.L. "Nutritional Conditioning." *Clinics in Sports Medicine* 3 (July 1984): 567—582.

22. Higdon, H. "Breakfast (Lunch and Dinner) of Champions." *Hippocrates* 2 (1988): 44—58-

23. Holloszy, J.O., M.J. Rennie, R.C. Hickson et al. "Physiologic Consequences of the Biochemical Adaptations to Endurance Exercise." *Ann. NY Acad. Sci.* 301 (1977): 440—450.

24. Ivy, J.L., D.L. Costill, J.W. Fink, and R.W. Lower. "Influence of Caffeine and Carbohydrate Feedings on Endurance Performance." *Med. and Science in Sports* 11 (1979): 6—11.

25. Ivy, J.L., A.L. Katz, C.L. Cutler et al. "Muscle Glycogen Synthesis After Exercise: Effect of Time of Carbohydrate Ingestion." *J. Appl. Physiol.* 64 (1988): 1480—1485-

26. Karlsson, J., and B. Saltin. "Diet, Muscle Glycogen, and Endurance Performance." *J. App. Phys.* 31 (1971): 203—206.

27. Larson, E.B., and R.A. Bruce. "Editorial: Exercise and Aging." *Ann. of Int. Med.* 105 (November 1986): 783—785.

28. Locksley, R. "Fuel Utilization in Marathons: Implications for Performance." *West. J. Med.* 133 (1980): 493—502.

29. Loy, S.F., R.K. Conlee, W.W. Winder, A.G. Nelson, D.A. Arnall, and A.G. Fisher. "Effects of 24 Hour Fast on Cycling Endurance Time at Two Different Intensities." *J. Appl. Physiol.* 61 (1986): 654—659.

30. Merkin, G. "Eating for Competition." *Seminars in Adolescent Medicine* 3 (1987): 177—183.

31. Meyers, F., and R.S. Fischer, "A Rational Approach to Gastric Emptying Disorders." *International Medicine* 9 (1988): 112—122.

32. Morella, J.J., and R.J. Turchetti. *Nutrition and the Athlete.* Van Nostrand Reinhold Company,1982.

33. Neufer, P.D., D.L. Costill, M.G. Flynn, J.P. Kirwan, J.B. Mitchell, and J. Houmard. "Improvements in Exercise Performance: Effects of Carbohydrate Feedings and Diet." *J. Appl. Physiol.* 62 (1987): 983—988.

34. Pena, N. "Legal Performance Enhancers," *Bicycling* 28 (July 1987): 30—34.

35. Pena, N. "What Does this Man Know that You Don't? " *Bicycling* 19 (1988): 73—77.

36. "Position of the American Dietetic Association: Nutrition for

Physical Fitness and Athletic Performance for Adults." *J. Am. Dietetic Assoc.* 87 (1987): 933—939.

37. Powers, S.K., R.J. Byrd, R. Tulley, and T. Calender. "Effects of Caffeine Ingestion on Metabolism and Performance During Graded Exercise." *Med. Sci. Sports Exer.* 14 (1982): 176.

38. Pritikin, N. *Diet for Runners.* New York: Simon and Schuster, 1982.

39. *Recommended Dietary Allowances.* National Academy of Sciences, 1980.

40. Roedde, S., J.D. MacDougall, J.R. Sutton, and H.J. Green. "Supercompensation of Muscle Glycogen in Trained and Untrained Subjects." *Canad J. Appl. Sports Sciences* 11 (1986): 42—46.

41. Schoene, R.B. "Nutrition for Ultra-endurance: Several Hours to Several Months," *Clinics in Sports Medicine* 3 (July 1984): 679—692.

42. Simons–Morton, B.G., R.R. Pate, and D.G. Simons–Morton. "Prescribing Physical Activity to Prevent Disease." *Postgraduate Medicine* 83 (1988): 165—176.

43. Smith, N.J. "Weight Control in the Athlete," *Clinics in Sports Medicine* 3 (July 1984): 693—704.

44. White, J., and M.A. Ford. "The Hydration and Electrolyte Maintenance Properties of an Experimental Sports Drink." *Brit. J. Sports Medicine* 17 (1983): 51—58.

45. White, J.A., C. Ward and H. Nelson. "Ergogenic Demands of a 24-Hour Cycling Event." *Brit. J. Sports Medicine* 18 (1984): 165—171.

46. Whitney, E.N. *Nutrition – Concepts and Controversies.* West Publishing Company, 1982.

47. Whitt, F.R., and D.G. Wilson. *Bicycling Science.* Cambridge: MIT Press, 1982.

48. Williams, M.H. "Vitamin and Mineral Supplements to Athletes: Do They Help?" *Clinics in Sports Medicine* 3 (July 1984): 623—637.

49. Wilmore, J.H., and B.J. Freund. "Nutritional Enhancement of Athletic Performance." *Current Concepts in Nutrition* 15 (1986): 67—97.

50. Young, V.R. "Protein and Amino Acid Metabolism in Relation to Physical Exercise." *Current Concepts in Nutrition* 15 (1986): 9—32.

51. Zahradnik, F. "Sports Drinks," *Bicycling* 28 (September 1987): 46—50.

52. Zanecosky, A. "Nutrition for Athletes." *Clinics in Podiatric Medicine and Surgery* 3 (1986): 623—630.

Glossary

Absolute work: The actual number of Calories expended to accomplish a task. It is the same for all individuals and not affected by the level of conditioning.

adenosine diphosphate (ADP): A coenzyme that acts as an intermediate carrier in cellular metabolism. It is transformed into ATP (see below) by the addition of a phosphate group.

adenosine triphosphate (ATP): An organic compound acting as a carrier for intermediary energy storage during cellular metabolism. It is the last chemical compound formed in the transfer of food energy into mechanical work.

aerobic metabolism: Cellular energy release carried out in the presence of oxygen.

anaerobic metabolism: Cellular energy release carried out without oxygen.

basal metabolic rate (BMR): The heat production (energy consumption) of an individual at the lowest level of cellular activity (metabolism) in the waking state.

bonk: A cyclists term for the fatigue that occurs after prolonged exertion, probably from exhaustion of muscle glycogen reserves. In running, this is referred to as 'the wall'.

caloric replacement: The number of Calories that must be eaten to replace those required to carry out a certain amount of work.

calorie: The old scientific unit of energy (superseded by the joule, see below). It is the energy required to raise the temperature of 1 gram of water 1 degree Centigrade.

Calorie: A unit of energy equal to 1000 calories. This is the unit used when referring to the energy content of foods as well as to the production and utilization of energy in man.

carbohydrate: An organic compound containing carbon, hydrogen, and oxygen. It is a basic source of energy for the cell and yields 4.1 Calories per gram.

cardiac output: The rate at which blood is pumped by the heart, usually expressed in liters/minute.

chyme: The semi-fluid mass of partly digested food passed from the stomach into the duodenum.

complex carbohydrate: An organic molecule composed of at least two simple (single) carbohydrate molecules.

concentration: The quantity of any substance in a defined volume of a solution or mixture.

disaccharide: A carbohydrate consisting of two molecules.

diuretic: A compound which promotes water excretion by the kidneys.

efficiency: The ratio of work output to energy input.

energy: The capacity for doing work.

essential: Necessary. In the context of nutrition, this refers to basic food elements (fats and amino acids) that cannot be synthesized by the body. These substances are each necessary for cellular metabolism and existence, making them also essential components of the diet.

exhaustion: The point at which the athlete cannot maintain an initial level of activity, even with an adequate blood glucose supply. Related to a change in the muscle itself — not the source of energy.

fatigue: The point at which the body's glucose stores are depleted and all energy is derived from fat metabolism. It can be reversed with oral glucose supplements.

fatty acid (FA): One of the molecules making up a triglyceride, the basic component of fatty tissue, and an essential intermediary in fat metabolism.

fluid deficit: The difference between the body's ideal water content and it's actual water content (usually after exercise).

fructose: Fruit sugar. Important, as it can be metabolised to glycogen without insulin.

gluconeogenesis: The production of glucose, a carbohydrate, from either fat or protein. It is often an intermediate step in energy production from these materials.

glucose: The monosaccharide which is the most important carbohydrate in cellular metabolism.

glycogen: The form in which carbohydrate is stored in the body. When needed, it is converted in the tissues into glucose.

joule: The scientific unit of energy — see the conversion table in Appendix B for the equivalent in calories and Calories.

international units: See under SI units.

lactic acid: One of the by-products of anaerobic metabolism. It has a negative effect on muscle functioning and, in this way, limits athletic performance.

maximal oxygen consumption ($\dot{V}O_{2max}$): The maximum amount (volume) of oxygen that an individual can consume in a set period of time (l/min). It can also be expressed per kilogram of body weight (ml/kg/min). It is a reflection of the upper limit of aerobic metabolism and is a product of the maximal cardiac output and maximal arterial-venous oxygen difference.

maximum heart rate (MHR): The maximum attainable heart rate for an individual. It decreases with age and can be estimated using the formula: MHR = 220 — (age in years).

metabolism: The biochemical cellular functions involved in energy production.

minerals: Inorganic elements or compounds that are essential constituents of all cells.

monosaccharide: A carbohydrate consisting of a single molecule.

osmotic activity: Relating to the concentration (number of molecules in a given volume) of a solution.

oxidation: Literally, the chemical combination with oxygen, releasing energy in the process.

oxygen consumption ($\dot{V}_{O2}$): The total volume of oxygen consumed by the cells of the body over a given period of time in carrying out the basic metabolic functions.

oxygen debt: The amount of oxygen required for the removal of the lactic acid and other metabolic products that accumulate during anaerobic metabolism.

paceline: Several bicyclists drafting (following closely) one another in a line to minimize energy needs and improve the performance of the group.

polymer: A substance made up of a chain of similar units. In the context of this text, it refers to a chain of simple glucose molecules.

power: The rate at which work is done. For example, if an 80 kg bicycle and rider are raised 3 meters in 1 minute, power is expressed as 240 kg-meters per minute (kgm/h).

relative work rate: The percentage of a person's $\dot{V}_{O2max}$ required to accomplish a task. Even though the absolute work is the same for all riders, the relative work rate can vary from individual to individual, depending on the level of conditioning.

second wind: The phenomenon of easing of effort for any given level of exercise which occurs after warming up. It is thought to relate, in some degree, to a shift from carbohydrate towards fat metabolism in the cell.

SI units (international units): The international system of units (as opposed to the English system) based on the metric system. In nutritional literature, the English system remains widely accepted in the US.

trace element: Any mineral supplied by the food that is only present in the body in a minute concentration.

triglyceride: The basic molecule of fat (adipose) tissue. Triglycerides contain 9.3 Calories per gram.

urea: The end product of protein metabolism in man, which is excreted.

work: The application of a force over a (vertical) distance. For example, moving 80 kg up over a distance of 2 meters equals 160 kg-meters (kgm) of work.

Index

Other Books from Bicycle Books, Inc.

Major Taylor

The extraordinary career of a champion bicycle racer
by Andrew Ritchie

304 pages plus 32-page photo insert
ISBN 0-933201-14-1, hardcover

The fascinating story of Major Taylor, the black American professional bicycle racer who was the world's most popular sportsman around the turn of the century.

The Bicycle Racing Guide

Technique and training for bicycle racers and triathletes
by Rob van der Plas

256 pages with over 250 illustrations
ISBN 0-933201-13-3, paperback

This is the most complete and authoritative guide to training for bicycle racing.

In High Gear

The world of professional bicycle racing
by Samuel Abt

192 pages text plus 16-page photo insert

ISBN 0-933201-24-5 Hardcover
ISBN 0-933201-25-7 Paperback

The inside story on the international bicycle racing scene and the life of the professional bike racer. This book is a must for anybody who follows bicycle racing as a spectator or a participant

The Bicycle Fitness Book

Using the bike for health and fitness
by Rob van der Plas

144 pages with over 80 illustrations
ISBN 0-933201-23-0, paperback

Cycle for fitness. This book shows exactly how to select the right gear how to ride and how to train.

The Mountain Bike Book

Choosing, riding and maintaining the off-road bicycle
by Rob Van der Plas

208 pages with 250 illustrations
ISBN 0-933201-18-4, paperback

The second edition of Bicycle Books' first title. Acknowledged to be the best book of its kind. Fully updated and expanded.

The Bicycle Repair Book

The complete manual of bicycle care
by Rob Van der Plas

140 pages with 300 illustrations
ISBN 0-933201-11-7, paperback

Easily the best general bicycle repair manual on the market today. This book is kept fully updated each time it is reprinted.

The Bicycle Touring Manual

Using the bicycle for touring and camping
by Rob Van der Plas

272 pages with over 250 illustrations
ISBN 0-933201-15-X, paperback

This book covers all aspects of touristic cycling, from selecting bike and other equipment to planning your route and finding the way both at home and abroad.

Mountain Bike Maintenance

Repairing and maintaining the off-road bicycle
by Rob Van der Plas

112 pages with over 120 illustrations
ISBN 0-933201-22-2

This new manual provides well illustrated step-by-step instructions for all the maintenance work on the ATB, or mountain bike.

Roadside Bicycle Repairs

The simple guide to fixing your bike
by Rob Van der Plas

112 pages with over 100 illustrations
ISBN 0-933201-16-8, paperback

This handy pocket-size book provides all the information needed to carry out necessary repairs while riding the bike. Ideal for the non-technically inclined.

The Bicycle Commuting Book

Using the bicycle for utility and transportation
by Rob Van der Plas

112 pages with over 80 illustrations
ISBN 0-9332201-29-X, paperback

This thorough manual on biking for transportation wraps up the author's 30 years of experience as a bicycle commuter. A superb companion for anyone who wants to use the bike as a means of transportation.

How to Order

All books published by Bicycle Books, Inc. may be obtained through the book or bike trade. If not available locally, order directly from the publisher. Allow three weeks for shipping. Mail coupon to:

Bicycle Books, Inc.
P. O. Box 2038
Mill Valley, CA 94941
Tel.:   (415) 381 O172
FAX: (415) 381 6912

Please enclose payment in full (check or money order made payable to Bicycle Books, Inc.) Books not paid for in advance will be sent UPS COD.

Canadian and other foreign customers please note:
All prices quoted are US $ prices and must be paid in advance with check drawn on US bank or International Money Order – no COD available on foreign orders. Shipping charge $2.50 (or $4.50 Air Mail) per book.

Please send the following book(s):   ☐   Check here if payment is enclosed

The Mountain Bike Book	_____ copies @	$8.95 =	$ _____
The Bicycle Repair Book	_____ copies @	$7.95 =	$ _____
The Bicycle Racing Guide	_____ copies @	$9.95 =	$ _____
The Bicycle Touring Manual	_____ copies @	$9.95 =	$ _____
Roadside Bicycle Repairs	_____ copies @	$3.95 =	$ _____
Major Taylor (hardcover)	_____ copies @	$19.95 =	$ _____
Bicycling Fuel	_____ copies @	$7.95 =	$ _____
Mountain Bike Maintenance	_____ copies @	$6.95 =	$ _____
In High Gear (hardcover)	_____ copies @	$16.95 =	$ _____
In High Gear (paperback)	_____ copies @	$10.95 =	$ _____
The Bicycle Fitness Book	_____ copies @	$7.95 =	$ _____
The Bicycle Commuting Book	_____ copies @	$7.95 =	$ _____

Sub total $ _____
California residents add 6 (6.5%) sales tax $ _____
Postage and handling $2.00 first book,
$1.00 each additional book (within US) $ _____

Total amount $ _____

Name:_____
Address:_____
City, state, zip: _____   Tel.: (_____) _____